I0531178

I CAN'T
BELIEVE
THEY LET
ME IN

Confronting Imposter Syndrome and

Letting Yourself In

CC NICHOLS

Copyright © 2025 by Rural Duke Productions.

All rights reserved.

No part of this work may be reproduced, stored in a retrieval system or transmitted in any form by any means, electronic, mechanical, photocopying, recording, or otherwise, without written permission of the publisher, except for the use of brief quotations in a book review.

ISBN Paperback: 979-8-9937909-0-9

ISBN E-book: 979-8-9937909-1-6

Cover design: Miracolo / 99Designs

Interior formatting: Mark Thomas / Coverness.com

To my adult children—This book is full of some of my many mistakes. I hope reading them helps you make fewer of your own and find self-acceptance and confidence long before I did.

TABLE OF CONTENTS

Introduction: The Moment They Finally Figured Me Out .... *i*

PART ONE: THE FRAUDULENT MIND *1*

    Chapter 1: Welcome to the Fraud Club *3*

    Chapter 2: The Stories We Tell Ourselves *16*

    Chapter 3: Your Brain Is Lying to You *31*

PART TWO: CONFRONTING IMPOSTER SYNDROME *49*

    Chapter 4: Perfectionism: The Hustle that Never Ends *51*

    Chapter 5: Putting Fear Back in the Box *70*

    Chapter 6: When Self-Doubt Turns into Self-Sabotage *84*

PART THREE: REFRAMING IMPOSTER SYNDROME *97*

    Chapter 7: The Secret Nobody Tells You *99*

    Chapter 8: Imposter Syndrome as a Superpower *119*

    Chapter 9: Your Greatest Hits (and Misses) *135*

    Chapter 10: Nobody Is Thinking about You (and That's a Good Thing) *146*

PART FOUR: LETTING YOURSELF IN *161*

    Chapter 11: Don't Believe Everything You Think *163*

    Chapter 12: Own the Room (Even When You Don't Feel Like It) *176*

    Conclusion: The Real You Was Never an Imposter *191*

References *195*

Acknowledgments *199*

About the Author *201*

INTRODUCTION

The Moment They Finally Figured Me Out

At any moment, I'm convinced someone will walk into the room, tap me on the shoulder, and announce:

"CC, we're sorry, but there's been a mistake. We've had someone dig into your past. They talked to your high school friends, Navy buddies, and coworkers from every job you've ever had."

"Oh," I'll reply, trying to look calm. "Those are some of my closest friends."

"Yes, and that's the problem. We don't like any of them—altogether a rather shady bunch. Now we know everything. We know about the sixth-grade homework assignment you claimed your dog ate. We know you spent most of your Navy career unclogging toilets on a ship with 800 other dudes. We know about your failed high school wrestling career and how you partied your way through much of your twenties. Oh, and your singer-songwriter side hustle? Let's not even start. Frankly, we're embarrassed. So again, we're sorry, but *you don't belong here.*"

"But I have an MBA, and my sales numbers are consistently at the top!" I'll protest.

"Yes, about that. Your education is from a state school, and honestly, we're pretty sure a monkey could hit those sales figures. So please pack up and leave. Security will escort you out."

The details may not match, but does the fear of being called out sound familiar? You're not alone. Studies show that up to 70 percent of people experience imposter syndrome. That includes some of the most successful and accomplished individuals in history.

You walk into a room, thinking you belong, and suddenly it's a courtroom. A prosecutor you didn't know existed is laying out your worst moments like evidence.

Exhibit A: the typo in that big email.

Exhibit B: the time you forgot your boss's name.

The gavel slams: guilty of being a fraud.

Or maybe it's a horror movie. You're taking a risk stepping up, and that shadowy voice you thought you had left behind is already waiting. *"Remember the last time you blew it? So do they."* That's how imposter syndrome works. It doesn't just show up—it scripts a whole disaster movie starring you. And it always premieres when you care the most.

That hollow feeling deep inside you? It's not proof you're broken. It's a message that you've hit the exact place where your potential is calling you to grow and shine. This book will help you see imposter syndrome for what it really is—not a stop sign but a signal you're on the right path. You'll learn how to reframe self-doubt into clarity, turn fear into fuel, and step into your actual strength with confidence and courage. Doubt's elimination isn't our purpose; you're here to move forward with it.

Because that's the trick. Imposter syndrome doesn't attack when you're coasting. It prefers moments of high stakes and deep care. A big meeting. A career leap. A dream you've decided to chase. Right when you care the most, it loves to bring along a highlight reel of every mistake, failure, and awkward moment you've ever had, amplifying your deepest fears.

And the worst part? It's convincing. Despite knowing you've earned your place, it feels as if you're moments away from being exposed.

Why does it do this? Because imposter syndrome snacks not only on doubt. It feasts on ambition. It thrives in the gap between where we are and where we're trying to go. That gap? It's not a sign of failure. It's a signal of growth. It's where courage is born, where progress begins, and where you're proving step by step that you belong. It's also where you'll find the tools to help you navigate what's ahead.

Here's what I have learned through mistake after mistake. That voice in your head isn't proof you're a fraud—it's proof you care. People who don't care don't lose sleep over getting it right. They don't push themselves into unfamiliar places. They don't feel the stretch marks of growth. *You do* because you're in the game and part of the action, not safely watching from the sidelines.

That's the real story imposter syndrome tries to hide. It shows up because you're doing something that matters. And together, I'm going to help you flip the script—to turn that nagging voice from a wrecking ball into a building block, to transform self-doubt into a secret weapon, fueling your courage instead of stealing it.

Whether you're chasing a promotion, launching a creative dream, stepping into a new role, or simply trying to believe you're enough right where you are—this journey is for you. And the best part? You're already braver than you think. You're already farther along than you know. Now—let's take back the remote and run the show.

But before we can change the story playing in our heads, we need to understand the one that's been running on a loop. Imposter syndrome doesn't just whisper doubts. It spins a full-blown narrative, complete with charts, evidence, and emotional landmines. It strikes exactly when the stakes are highest, hitting the tender places where we care the most. Worst of all, the voice doesn't shout like an obvious villain. It blends in, speaking with enough familiarity to masquerade as truth. Over time the lines blur. We stop questioning it … until we believe it as gospel. But that voice isn't reality. It's a liar, and it's long past time we called it out.

Recognizing the absurdity of imposter syndrome—wherein every success you achieve feels accidental and every mistake feels like proof you don't belong—is the first step to loosening its grip. And the fact that you're reading this means the process has already begun.

Through reflective exercises, relatable examples, and strategies tested by others who have walked this path, you'll gain clarity and confidence to tackle imposter syndrome head-on, like identifying your "success blind spots" and creating a roadmap for tackling moments of doubt.

I Can't Believe They Let Me In isn't here to teach you how to silence that voice (you can't). Self-doubt is part of being human, especially when you're pushing yourself to grow. While you can't eliminate it, you can learn to stop letting it run the show. Think of this as a roadmap for turning imposter syndrome into a tool for self-growth.

We'll also redefine what success looks like—not as perfection but as showing up, messy and real. Doubt won't vanish, but your relationship with it will change. You'll recognize your inner critic not as a sign you're broken but as proof that you're stepping into the life you actually want.

This is your time to step out from under the shadow of self-doubt and into a mindset where growth, courage, and imperfection can coexist. After all, nobody needs another year of feeling as if their Zoom call mishap is a disqualifying life event. (Forgetting to unmute yourself shouldn't haunt you forever.)

I Can't Believe They Let Me In is your guide to taking the first step today. With tools, strategies, and stories, you'll see that you've always had what it takes to move forward when self-doubt tries to hold you back. Whether you're chasing a big dream, stepping into a new role, or trying to feel at ease in your own skin, this book will help you see yourself for what you are—enough.

PART ONE

THE FRAUDULENT MIND

CHAPTER 1

Welcome to the Fraud Club

Have you ever found yourself in a room questioning your place regardless of how hard you worked to get there? You know the moment. Doubt shows up without warning and taps you on the shoulder. Maybe it hits during a meeting, on your first day in a new role, or after you speak up in a room full of sharp minds. You glance around, waiting for someone to ask, "How did *you* get in?"

Welcome to the Fraud Club. Everyone gets in the same way: by caring too much. You care about getting it right, being enough, not dropping the ball, and about nine thousand other things. That's what opens the door.

Here's the twist: this club includes almost everyone. And we have awards:

- **Champion Overthinker:** For rerunning every conversation in your head until the sun comes up.
- **Sweat-Stained Speaker Award:** For white-knuckling your way through a presentation while your shirt exposes your nervous truth.
- **Mind Reader Merit Badge:** For assuming everyone else sees your mistakes the moment you make them. (Spoiler: They don't.)

Sound familiar? Then you're one of us. You're not broken. You're human and in good company.

The Catch-22 of Confidence

Imposter syndrome runs on a cruel logic. If you doubt yourself, it must mean you're unqualified. But if you don't, then you must be blind to your flaws. Either way, the voice in your head calls you a fraud.

It's a rigged loop. No matter what you do, you lose.

Joseph Heller captured this trap in *Catch-22*. During deadly bombing runs, a pilot could stop flying missions only if he were insane. But if he *asked* to be grounded, that request proved he was sane—so he had to keep flying. There was no escape. Imposter syndrome works the same way. If you question your place, it must mean you don't belong. If you don't, then you must be too blind to see the truth. Either way, the voice convinces you that you're a fraud. You spin your wheels and stay stuck.

These aren't exceptions. They're reminders. Self-doubt doesn't chase the weak. It follows the ones who care the most.

Introspection

When have you doubted yourself most, and what might that say about how much you care?

That inner critic loves to show up when you're stretching toward something that matters. It feeds off the gap between where you are and where you're going. The more you grow, the louder it gets.

But here's the shift: that voice isn't proof you don't belong. It's a signal that you're on the edge of growth. People who don't care don't wrestle with doubt. You wrestle with doubt because you do care.

That matters.

Next, let's talk about why high-pressure spaces make this voice louder and why you're not the only one hearing it.

Introspection

Think about a recent moment when self-doubt crept in. What story did your inner critic tell you? How did it affect your choices?

When the Stakes Are High (And the Velociraptors Are Circling)

Imposter syndrome does not wait in the background. It stalks you the moment the stakes rise. Step up, speak out, or aim high, and the brush moves. Something is watching.

Think *Jurassic Park*. You walk into a new space, steady yourself, and try to blend in by nodding with a smile. You believe you might pull it off. Then something shifts. A question comes from the side. A glance lingers too long. You freeze. That voice in your head starts again. You look around and wonder if everyone else attended the "man-eating, no-longer-extinct dinosaur survival class" while you wandered into the arena without a clue.

You expected a calm room. Instead, a T-Rex breathes down your neck, and every cell in your body braces for impact.

Self-doubt doesn't chase apathy. It circles the ones who stretch toward something bigger. Classrooms. Boardrooms. Interviews. Performance reviews. Wherever people strive to do well, imposter syndrome prowls. The pressure doesn't create it—it calls it out.

Ambition draws it in. The moment you reach past comfort, the voice speaks up: *You don't belong. You're not ready. Someone will figure it out.*

I've felt this in casual conversations and around dinner tables. But nowhere does the ground feel more unstable than at work. That's where the pressure builds, where performance becomes public, and where your inner critic sharpens its claws.

One moment stands out. I was prepping a senior executive for a client meeting that could shift everything. My job? Steer the conversation, back him up, and keep things on track. On paper, I checked every box. In my head I crouched in the tall grass, waiting for the velociraptor to devour me limb by limb.

Let me take you there and show you the path that led me into that tall grass.

From Navy Toilets to Boardrooms

I'm proud of my time in the Navy. It gave me the chance to see the world, build lifelong friendships, and shape who I am today. A large part of my actual job onboard the *USS Camden*? Unclogging toilets used by 800 other guys. Glamorous? Not even close. Picture me with a wrench in hand, ankle deep in a flooded head, trying to convince a clogged pipe to surrender.

Fast-forward a few years. I graduated from college and landed my first pharmaceutical sales job. My path had come full circle. Now I was pitching a prescription laxative to gastroenterologists. My career had jumped from clearing pipes to helping people clear *their* pipes. An upgrade? Sure. An example of life's irony? Sure. As I made my first sales call, standing in a doctor's office and trying to convince a physician with years of medical training that my bowel prep would change the game, I thought, *At least I'm not ankle-deep in sewage with a plunger in my hand.*

My new suit and tie replaced my Navy dungarees and waterlogged boots, but I still did not feel worthy of the job. Picture a twenty-something with zero science background standing in a medical office, trying to look as if he belonged. My manager hovered nearby, eyes locked on me, ready to pounce at the first mistake. My palms sweated, my heart pounded, and my brain looped through every way this could fall apart.

I walked up to the receptionist and introduced myself. She did not call security, which felt like a win. She led us to the sample closet, a cramped and dusty room with all the charm of a forgotten storage shed. That is where my manager launched into a crash course in gastroenterology. Polyethylene glycol: improved flavor, earlier polyp detection, lifesaving benefits. All solid points, all things I was supposed to remember from training.

Inside that tiny room, my brain checked out. Everything I had learned disappeared. My manager's voice blurred into background noise, as with the teacher from *Peanuts*. Wah-wah wah.

When the doctor finally walked in, he gave me a glance that said, "I have three minutes—go." My manager stepped back. I stood alone.

I extended my shaky hand, swallowed the lump in my throat, and searched my brain for anything. Nothing. I could not remember a single product feature. Basic small talk escaped me. I blanked on the name of my company, the product, and yes, I forgot my own name. Finally, I pulled myself together and stammered, "Umm....ahh...samples?"

He signed the form without a word and walked out.

I stood there, sweaty and mortified, as my manager escorted my stunned self back to the car. I'm sure he gave me some much-needed feedback. I don't remember any of it. And I doubt I heard much of it while he was saying it. After surviving a T. Rex encounter, I was in shock. For reasons I still don't understand, he did not fire me, a mercy I came to appreciate only much later.

Things didn't turn around overnight. There wasn't one big win. It was a slow build of small, gritty moments. Over time I asked better questions, recovered faster from the stumbles, and stopped clenching the steering wheel during every ride-along. Physicians started listening. A few asked for my opinion. Promotions came (never flashy, always earned), and with each new territory or role, a little more confidence followed. I moved into positions that blended strategy, storytelling, and helping people navigate complex decisions. By the time I stepped into that boardroom, what I brought to the table wasn't just knowledge—it was a career built on persistence, pattern recognition, and the quiet competence that doesn't need applause to be real.

What the C-Suite Taught Me

Twenty-five years after that sweaty moment in the sample closet, I had built a career in sales and marketing. I had learned to navigate clinical conversations, guide complex meetings, and to admit when I didn't know something. Self-doubt hadn't left—it had evolved.

One moment reminded me of how imposter syndrome sticks around, no matter your title.

Our new chief commercial officer joined the company with a résumé that read like a "Who's Who" of the pharmaceutical industry. He had climbed through some of the biggest names in the industry and looked like someone who had everything figured out. But two weeks into the job, he was still learning the ropes of new systems, products, and customer dynamics.

One of those customers was Dr. Thomas, a nationally recognized physician who had spent decades researching the diseases we helped treat. The man knew everything. He had published extensively, spoken at global conferences, and delivered it all with the ease and charisma of a movie star. His nurse practitioner, Nancy, ran the place. She tracked every detail, anticipated questions, and translated clinical complexity into action. Together, they were an unstoppable pair.

Before the meeting, the CCO and I prepped over Zoom. He turned to me and said, "If the conversation gets too clinical, feel free to jump in and steer me back."

That moment stopped me. Here was a leader at the top of the chain admitting he didn't know everything. He didn't bluff. He didn't posture. He asked for help and gave me permission to help.

And the meeting? It went smoothly. He stuck to what he knew, asked smart questions, and handed the conversation over to me when the science got deep. My job was to guide the flow and help him shine. By the end, Dr. Thomas had shared valuable insights, and the CCO had earned trust by staying grounded.

That experience taught me something huge. Imposter syndrome doesn't fade as you rise. It changes shape. The difference is in how you respond. The CCO didn't let self-doubt control the room. He named it, worked around it, and relied on his team. That wasn't weakness. It was wisdom.

Imposter syndrome shows up whether you pitch bowel prep to your first doctor or walk into a boardroom with a global expert. It doesn't care about your title or experience. The voice still sneaks in. That doesn't mean you have to believe it.

The goal isn't to erase doubt—it's working with it. Ask for help. Play to your strengths. And remember: being in the room means you earned your spot.

Still, that inner voice pops up at the worst times. But I've learned to see it for what it is: a sign that I care, a signal that I'm growing.

Introspection

What's one strength you bring to the table that no one else can replicate? How has it made a difference in your life or work?

Music, Meaning, and Shaky Hands

Imposter syndrome does not stop at the office. It barges into the parts of life we care about most. For me, that part is music.

Music has always been more than a hobby to me. It gives me a place to breathe. As a kid, I could not make sense of the world around me. Adults spoke in riddles I did not understand. But when I put on headphones and pressed "play" on that revolutionary Walkman from the 1980s, everything settled. I got lost in the lyrics. The Police. U2. Def Leppard. The Rolling Stones. Their songs gave shape to chaos.

I leaned into heavy guitars and pounding drums. Iron Maiden. AC/DC. Twisted Sister. That sound covered my doubts like armor. Then, at the age of fifteen, my best friend, Jason, handed me a Bob Dylan cassette, and the world shifted. The lyrics cut more deeply than anything else I had heard. Dylan said things I had only felt.

From Dylan we found John Prine and other storytellers. The music slowed down. The words took over. I listened and connected.

By my senior year of high school, the urge to make music had grown stronger. My dad brought home a guitar for me, and I signed up for lessons. Chords refused to form. Theory bounced off my brain. Focus lasted about as long as a pop song intro. The fact that I could not match Eric Clapton after fifteen minutes of practice drove my reward-hungry brain up the wall. But I kept at it, on and off. The playing never got great, but it stuck. Not skill, not polish—just persistence. I kept going for years.

Then, around the age of thirty, I picked up the banjo. Something clicked.

My hands found the rhythm. My ears caught the patterns. I ventured into attempting the fiddle, an instrument that exaggerates every mistake, and kept going. Alone in my house I could play. Music became a source of joy again. It belonged to me.

Until someone else walked in.

The moment I had an audience, everything fell apart. My hands shook. My timing disappeared. The Fraud Fairy stormed in and yelled, "You'll never be Béla Fleck, so why try?"

The joy disappeared. I shut down. I told myself I was not good enough. The same voice that once crept into meetings now crept into music.

That moment helped me see it clearly. Doubt doesn't show up to shame our weakness—it shows up to challenge our love for something. The more something matters, the louder the voice gets.

Over time I kept playing—not for praise, not for perfection, just for me. The voice still speaks, but I no longer believe it.

Turns out, it's not the stage that matters. It's what you feel when you step onto it.

Looking back, I see how often self-doubt tried to steal the joy from something I loved. Sometimes it won. But not every time. I kept playing because it mattered to me.

The voice saying, "You don't belong," loves to show up in moments that matter. That voice follows more than people like me. It shadows the best in the world—which tells us something crucial: doubt isn't proof you're not enough. It's proof you're doing something that *means* something.

Famous Members of the Fraud Club

Imposter syndrome doesn't play favorites. It cuts across industries, eras, and achievements. If you've ever doubted yourself, congratulations! You're in excellent company.

Champions with Doubts

Sports might seem like the ultimate proving ground, but many of the greatest athletes battle self-doubt.

Take **Jackie Joyner-Kersee,** often hailed as one of the greatest athletes of all time. She won six Olympic medals in track and field. Yet she spoke openly about battling nerves, asthma, and the pressure to prove herself every time she stepped on the track. Her story shows that world champions can carry self-doubt to the starting line.

Then there's **Muhammad Ali,** the heavyweight champion known for declaring, "I am the greatest." Behind the bravado, though, he admitted to fears about living up to his own words and wondered if he could deliver when it mattered most. The most confident voices can carry quiet doubt.

Billie Jean King, the tennis legend who broke barriers both on and off the court, felt the weight of proving herself long after her success. "Pressure is a privilege," she said. That's the flip side of imposter syndrome. It shows you care enough to want to rise to the occasion.

Creativity and Self-Doubt

The arts are a breeding ground for imposter syndrome. Why? Because creativity is personal, and validation can feel fleeting.

Consider **Lady Gaga,** who despite redefining pop culture and selling millions of records, admitted, "I still sometimes feel like a loser kid in high school." If someone with her level of global success can wrestle with doubt, the rest of us are in good company.

Maya Angelou, one of the most celebrated writers of the 20th century, admitted, "I have written eleven books, but each time I think, 'Uh-oh. They're going to find me out.'" If her genius wasn't enough to silence self-doubt, maybe the problem isn't us. It's the lie that imposter syndrome tells.

John Steinbeck, who won a Nobel Prize in Literature, once wrote in his journal, "I am not a writer. I've been fooling myself and other people." At the height of his career, he doubted his own talent, proof that self-doubt can shadow the most celebrated voices.

Agatha Christie, the queen of mystery novels, doubted her own abilities. "I don't think I can write at all," she once said, despite being one of the best-selling authors in history.

And **Neil Gaiman**, celebrated author of *Coraline* and *American Gods*, recalled attending a gathering of brilliant individuals and feeling out of place: "I just looked around and thought, 'I don't know why I'm here. They've made a terrible mistake.'" A fellow attendee reassured him, saying, "The trick is that no one here knows what they're doing. They just have great confidence."

Questioning Genius

Imposter syndrome doesn't limit itself to artistic spaces. It flourishes in academia and science, where constant testing of intellect and expertise occurs.

Albert Einstein, the father of modern physics, once called himself an "involuntary swindler," convinced that his fame outstripped his actual contributions. Let that sink in. The man who gave us the theory of relativity doubted his impact. If Einstein felt this way, maybe imposter syndrome is more about perception than reality.

Sonia Sotomayor, the first Latina Supreme Court justice, admitted in her memoir that she often felt out of place while at the height of her career. She once shared, "I have spent my years since Princeton, while at law school and in my various professional jobs, not feeling completely a part of the worlds I inhabit." For people at the top, self-doubt still lingers.

Charles Darwin, whose work reshaped our understanding of biology, often worried that he didn't deserve his place in history, believing others overestimated him. The greats question their worth. It's not proof of fraudulence. It's proof they cared.

The Weight of Leadership

Imposter syndrome isn't exclusive to creative or intellectual fields. It also thrives in high-stakes corporate environments.

Howard Schultz, the former CEO of Starbucks, confessed to doubting his vision when pitching the idea of a global coffeehouse chain. At one point he described feeling like "a kid with no college education" sitting in a room of professionals who seemed to have it all figured out.

Sheryl Sandberg, former COO of Meta (Facebook), wrote in *Lean In* about the moments she felt like a fraud. Her vulnerability encouraged others to see their own doubts as part of the journey, not a sign of failure.

Neil Armstrong was the first moonwalker. You would think that achievement alone would silence any self-doubt. Instead, Armstrong downplayed the moment, saying, "I was just the pilot. This was a collective effort, and I happened to be the one picked to step out first." Redefining history didn't shield him from questioning his significance.

Leading through Doubt

History's most iconic leaders wrestled with self-doubt. **Winston Churchill**, who led Britain through World War II, often questioned his abilities and battled depression. Yet his resolve and stirring speeches inspired a nation to persevere.

Joan of Arc, a teenage girl with no military training, led French forces to crucial victories in the Hundred Years' War. She faced constant skepticism (from others and herself), but her courage changed the course of history.

Their stories prove doubt doesn't define greatness; determination does. If they could press forward, so can you.

The Common Thread

What connects a Supreme Court justice, a pop icon, a physicist, and a punk rocker? Not their résumés. Not their personalities. Every one of them has heard that voice say, "You're not enough."

Imposter syndrome does not check credentials. It shows up for the high achievers, the quiet creatives, the world-changers, and the record-breakers. It does not care how many awards sit on the shelf or how many headlines carry your name.

If you've ever walked into a room and wondered, *How did I get here?* you're not an outlier. You're part of a very crowded club.

The people we admire most have felt this too. They kept showing up anyway.

You're in the Room for a Reason

Which brings us back to *you*. To reiterate, imposter syndrome doesn't come from weakness—it comes from caring. That voice in your head saying, *You don't belong,* doesn't speak up when you're coasting. It speaks up when the stakes rise, when the moment matters, when you care about doing well.

We've followed it through my personal journey in boardrooms, banjo lessons, bathrooms on a Navy ship, and a closet full of colonoscopy samples. We've seen it knock on the doors of elite athletes, world-class artists, justices, scientists, and CEOs. It does not care how many trophies or degrees you collect. It wants you to question whether you deserve them.

That is the trap, the catch-22 of confidence. If you doubt yourself, it must mean you don't belong. If you *don't* doubt yourself, it must mean you're blind to your flaws. Either way, the voice insists you are wrong. But what if that voice *isn't* there to destroy you? What if it is there to signal something else?

Think back to the chief commercial officer. He could have faked it. He could have pretended to know more than he did. But he didn't. He named what he didn't know and trusted his team to fill in the gaps. That wasn't failure. That was leadership.

Or the music. Playing alone brought joy. Sharing it brought fear—not because the music stopped mattering but because it mattered too much.

Despite that, we keep going. We raise our hands in meetings. We show up to new roles. We walk into rooms that make us sweat. Not because we feel fearless—but because we move forward anyway.

Imposter syndrome will always try to corner you into silence. But you don't have to play by its rules. You can step forward. You can speak up. You can stay in the room.

If you're in the room, it is not by accident.

You belong.

Next we'll look at why this voice exists, where it comes from, why it gets louder at the worst times, and how to stop it from running the show.

CHAPTER 2

The Stories We Tell Ourselves

Do you remember the first time you felt out of your depth? Not nervous but *exposed*. Maybe it was a Little League game, a school recital, or your first day on the job when you smiled too much and held your coffee as though it came with instructions.

For me it was 1978 on a Pee Wee football team in Ridgeley, West Virginia. One moment I was a scrawny six-year-old with gridiron dreams swirling around an oversized helmet. The next I was staring up at the sky, fused into the dirt, wondering how I was going to survive the next play and the rest of my entire life.

The Ridgeley Blackhawks were legendary, and somehow I had stumbled into their hallowed ranks. Not because of talent. That's what young boys did in Ridgeley. You played football. You became a Blackhawk. Wearing the black-and-white jersey wasn't some fall sport. It was a rite of passage with an enormous responsibility to succeed for the community.

They weren't just a team. They were the pint-sized pride of our entire town. Grit, tradition, and gridiron glory crammed into the inflated egos of elementary school boys. I was undersized for my age. My helmet slipped down over my eyes every play and worked against my ability to see anything from the sides. Was it safe? No. My body was the wrong size for the equipment. And the equipment seemed offended by my desire to wear it.

None of that mattered, though. I was a Ridgeley Blackhawk. I wore the uniform with my friends, who were all bigger than me and hit like semi-trucks. My dad had once stood on that same field. Now it was my turn to carry the legacy—or so I told myself, as I tried keeping my head attached to my shoulders.

A few years earlier, in 1975, the Blackhawks had achieved immortality. Back then they were the Ridgeley High School Blackhawks, and they had won our area's first state championship. Grown men still recited those plays like scripture. That story ended when Ridgeley High closed and merged with Fort Ashby to form Frankfort High. The old building reopened as Ridgeley Elementary and Middle School. The big Blackhawks were gone. Only the Pee Wee team remained to carry the name and the burden/glory.

I began my illustrious football career with all the enthusiasm of a baby bird jumping out of the nest for the very first time, confident that my underdeveloped wings would save me from the harsh ground. The very first practice shattered my NFL dreams. The collisions weren't only physical—they hit something deeper. They exploded through my emotional wiring like a system overload. My first tackling drill taught me two things: six-year-olds are unforgiving assassins, and my strict diet of SpaghettiOs had not prepared me for combat. The other kids seemed born for the game. They were fast, fearless, and raised on something heartier than canned pasta. I, meanwhile, spent most of practice eating dirt and searching for my dignity.

But I didn't quit. Not because I was brave—but because quitting wasn't an option. In our corner of Appalachia, toughness was mandatory. Football wasn't a pastime. It was a proving ground. You suited up, took the hits, and got back in line. Suggesting otherwise meant risking the dreaded label: *soft*.

Week after week I donned my oversized gear, ran all the wind sprints, did all the pushups, and embraced my role as a real-life tackling dummy. Then came an actual game.

At some point in the game the coach called an "end around" play. I don't remember the score. I don't remember the quarter. But I remember exactly what happened during that play and the one that followed.

For anyone unfamiliar, an "end around" is a bit of misdirection. The player lined up at the end of the offensive formation loops back toward the quarterback, takes the handoff, and races around the opposite side of the line. It's uncommon because its success hinges on surprise.

Here, the surprise wasn't the play. It was the person they handed the ball to.

Me.

I was the smallest kid on the field. Maybe the smallest kid in the state for my age. No one on the offense, defense, in the stands, or within the town's two-mile radius could have imagined they would hand the ball to me.

And that was the trick.

When the quarterback handed off the ball, my mind froze, and my feet kept turning. The weight of every parent, coach, and teammate's eyes fell on me. Flight or fight kicked in. I ran like a terrified fawn trying to avoid rabid coyotes. I turned the corner, dodged a lunging defender, and scurried for twelve yards before an angry linebacker took me down. A first down. A miracle. The cheers rang in my ears, bouncing around my helmet like fireworks. For one glorious moment I wasn't the runt. I was the hero.

Then the coach ran another trick play. Determined to outsmart the other team, he called the same play again.

This time the defense wasn't confused. They were furious. How could they let the smallest kid on the field get past them? They would not let that happen again.

At the very moment the quarterback handed me the ball, the same linebacker who had tackled me twelve yards downfield came crashing through and buried me eight yards behind the line of scrimmage while the ball flung out of my hands. He fused me with the cold, hard ground and then recovered the ball I had dropped. The impact crushed my chest and the loss of the ball crushed my sense of self. The cheers disappeared. I tasted dirt and stared at the sky, convinced that I saw cartoon birds circling my helmet. One minute I was the hero, the next—the undersized picky-eating kid I had always been.

After that, the coaches kept me far from the ball during practice and games. No complaints from me. I had become the team's unofficial tackling dummy. I suited up, took the hits, and tried not to die. My contribution was presence, not performance.

Looking back, I know that season taught me something about Newton's Second Law of Motion—smaller masses experience a much greater impact when hit by something heavier moving fast.

But the real lesson went deeper than physics.

Not belonging hurts in a way that no collision ever could.

Everyone else seemed stronger, faster, better. That feeling stuck. I didn't have the language for it then, but it was the first whisper of imposter syndrome, the quiet suspicion you've been let in by mistake and someone's going to figure it out.

The Pee Wee Blackhawks taught more than football. They enforced the unwritten rules of our Appalachian town. Toughness wasn't just respected—it was required. Conformity was the currency of worth. Vulnerability was weakness. In that space the seeds of doubt took root, not because I had failed but because I had tried and it still didn't feel like enough. In Appalachia, trying wasn't enough. You had to endure. The message wasn't "Do your best." It was "Don't show weakness." That not only shaped how I acted, but it also rewired what I believed about effort, failure, and worth.

Introspection

When did you first feel you didn't belong? Not in a dramatic,
movie-moment way—just that quiet, sinking sense that everyone
else had the playbook and you didn't.
What did you tell yourself to fit in? What did you believe?

The mistake on the field wasn't only a kid's fumble. It was a snapshot of how self-doubt begins. We don't focus on the twelve-yard gain. We zero in on the hit that knocked us down in the backfield. Whether it's a missed promotion or a relationship gone sideways, the failures speak louder than the progress.

That's how imposter syndrome starts—not in adulthood but in these brief moments of youthful uncertainty. It feeds on silence and grows through repetition. For me, it started on that field, buried under a helmet and a story I wanted to live up to.

But it wasn't really about football. That pattern of celebrating too little and fixating too much on flaws followed me into classrooms, workplaces, relationships, and everything in between. The uniform changed. The doubt stayed.

It wasn't *my* internal struggle. It reflected the world around me. That world measured worth by toughness, mistook confidence for competence, and defined success as never showing weakness. Although unwritten, someone enforced the rules daily.

And those rules? They show up everywhere.

This isn't unique to my little town in Appalachia. Our entire culture celebrates achievement and punishes imperfection. Most of us don't realize we've absorbed that message until we choke on it.

These early experiences not only shaped how I saw myself but also formed the blueprint for a belief system many of us inherit.

The Stories We Believe

Imposter syndrome starts early. It grows from the messages we hear and the rules we follow without realizing it. It feeds on the pressure to measure up before we know what the stakes are.

In my town toughness ruled everything. People respected grit more than any other virtue. They expected you to push through pain and never flinch. Vulnerability meant weakness. Silence seemed safer than honesty.

Football set the standard. Score—and you mattered. Miss a play—and no one remembered your name. The message came through fast. Fear had no place. Eyes stayed forward. Head stayed down. Approval became the goal. Belonging became the prize.

That mindset didn't stay on the field. It followed me into school and home. I thought success might protect me from rejection. I believed the pain made me less. Maybe your story looks different. But maybe the pressure feels the same. You had to earn your place. You had to get it right before anyone could trust you.

Robert Greene describes these beliefs as invisible scripts in *The Laws of Human Nature*. They take root before we notice. No one hands them to us. We absorb them through what people reward and what they ignore. They form when a parent praises toughness but stays silent when we show fear. They take shape in classrooms where only the loudest students get attention. These scripts teach us what earns acceptance and what invites rejection. Over time we stop asking where the rules came from and follow them without pause. We don't speak them out loud, but they guide what we say, what we hide, and what we believe we need to become.

Greene illustrates this idea through the life of Pericles, a leader in ancient Athens. In Athens they raised Pericles to value emotional intensity: boldness, drama, and quick reactions. But his mentor, the philosopher Anaxagoras, taught him to slow down, observe, and master his emotions. Instead of reacting on impulse, Pericles learned to step back, reflect, and respond with calmness. This mindset helped him stand apart from other leaders. While others chased applause, he relied on restraint. His early training shaped his leadership, not through lectures but through example and reward. That is how invisible scripts form. And that is also how one can rewrite them.

Invisible scripts are like the song "Wannabe," by the Spice Girls. Whether you like that song or not does not matter. But I guarantee you: The line "I'll tell you what I want, what I really, really want" has been stuck in your head at some point in life. And it wasn't invited. It slid its way into your brain like an unwanted worm and stuck around way past its welcome. That's how cultural messages work too. We absorb the chorus of "Don't speak up" or "You earn a seat only if you prove your perfection," and it plays on repeat beneath every decision. The challenge is changing the station to a song you wrote. Because until you do, those lying lyrics keep shaping your sense of who you are.

That's not an abstract concept. It was the Appalachian code. Keep your head down. Don't complain. Work twice as hard to prove you belong. For a kid like me, that meant internalizing every stumble as evidence I wasn't enough. Unlike Pericles, I didn't have the philosopher Anaxagoras guiding me. I had a community that rewarded silence and survival. My script told me to prove my value through achievement. It told me to hide anything soft. That mindset worked for a while. It got me through hard moments. But it also locked me into a version of myself that never felt secure.

Speaking up felt risky, especially in rooms that rewarded fast talk and bold claims. Quiet never meant passive. Holding back wasn't about fear. It became a reflex as I watched and listened. I noticed things others missed. But the longer I stayed silent, the more I questioned my place. Doubt crept in. Confidence looked like something I didn't recognize: loud, fast, certain. Anything softer seemed invisible.

When I read *Quiet,* by Susan Cain, something clicked. She didn't just describe what it feels like to hang back; she explained why people like me question our place. *Quiet* lays out how modern life rewards the fast responders, the group leaders, the ones who dominate the conversation. Schools praise students who speak first. Workplaces reward the loudest ideas in the room, not always the most thoughtful. Introverts learn early that presence alone is not enough. So we push harder. We will prepare more. We overcompensate to match the volume, not the value.

Cain calls this the "extrovert ideal," a belief that success belongs to the outgoing, the bold, the energetic. It's the cultural script that tells you to speak up or fall behind. That script teaches people like me to treat our natural quiet as a problem to fix. And when the world sends that message often enough, it sounds like truth.

That pressure creates a situation in which it's easy to doubt yourself. It tells you to become someone else to survive.

But what if that voice in your head isn't yours? What if someone else taught you to think that way?

You don't need to keep living by those scripts. You get to write new ones. Letting go of old stories isn't easy. But it's the only way to make space for something true.

Introspection

What rules did you grow up with?
Who did you believe you had to become?

The Extrovert Ideal

Susan Cain's book *Quiet* revealed a truth I had sensed for years. The world rewards boldness over reflection. It praises the voice that fills a room, not the one that pauses to think. From classrooms to boardrooms, people expect confidence to look loud, fast, and certain. If you don't match that image, you get passed over or left out.

As a kid, I felt that disappearing was never an option. Blending in required effort. Conversations moved fast, and keeping up took work. Humor offered a way through. A well-timed joke could distract from nerves and dodge attention. Sarcasm and self-deprecation became armor—not for protection from others but from the risk of being seen for who I was. Laughter became the shortcut to connection, sometimes at the cost of honesty. The performance became routine. It worked, but it left a question echoing in the quiet: Was the laugh for me or for the version of me I thought people wanted?

I remember watching kids who could take over a room without thinking twice. They moved through the day as if they owned every space they entered. Meanwhile, I rehearsed punchlines and watched reactions. Laughter felt like proof I belonged. But when the room emptied, doubt took over. Was I funny or simply afraid to show anything else?

Cain's writing helped me understand that this pressure doesn't stop with public speaking or leadership roles. It reaches into your identity, tells you to edit yourself, and convinces you that quiet means invisible and stillness means failure. That message becomes a script. You follow it without question.

This cultural pressure affects not only introverts. Extroverts face it too, in different ways. The script tells them to stay "on" all the time, to stay confident when they feel lost, to lead when they want or need to step back. While introverts worry about being overlooked, extroverts carry the fear of being exposed.

Think about the team leader who always knows what to say, the one who keeps meetings moving and fills every silence. That person might carry doubts that he or she never voices, feeling pressure to keep the show going when the confidence runs out. Or take the outgoing friend who makes everyone laugh. You would never guess that person lies awake wondering if people would accept the quieter version of him or her.

This is what Cain calls the "extrovert ideal." It sets a standard that feels impossible for most people. For introverts, the challenge is showing up in spaces that reward speed and dominance. For extroverts, the challenge is stepping away from the role they feel trapped inside.

The struggle looks different, but the cause often looks the same. We measure ourselves by standards we didn't create. We chase an idea of confidence that leaves little room for doubt, stillness, or rest. Imposter syndrome feeds on that chase. It grows in the gap between who we are and who we think we need to become.

But that gap isn't a flaw—it's a clue. Something inside you already knows the role doesn't fit. That's where the work begins.

Why Everyone's Faking It

Invisible scripts don't exist in isolation. They're reinforced by cultural messages about success, productivity, and worth. Together they create a world where self-doubt is expected. When society rewards perfection and punishes vulnerability, it's no wonder imposter syndrome takes root and grows.

These messages whisper through every space we enter. A surgeon questions his or her place because of not having attended a top medical school despite years of experience. A first-generation college student walks into a classroom and wonders if he or she belongs next to peers who inherited their places. An artist scrolls through social media and decides his or her work isn't good enough, based on likes and filtered images. These aren't random insecurities. They're shaped by the standards we absorb, often before we know we've agreed to them.

Perfectionism tells us that worth equals performance. It says we can't make mistakes if we want to belong. We learn to measure ourselves by external praise and constant output. Social media intensifies this. We scroll past curated success, comparing our behind-the-scenes to someone else's highlight reel. In the workplace the unspoken rule that confidence equals competence pushes people to act certain—despite their doubts.

For the entire history of man, society after society and person after person has confused confidence with competence. We reward the person who speaks with authority, not always the one who's right. That kind of distortion pushes us to perform rather than engage, to hide our learning curve instead of embracing it.

The problem affects more than certain jobs or personality types. These scripts show up across industries and identities. They tell us to prove ourselves over and over again, to earn belonging, to chase achievement, to look polished when we're struggling. Because these standards feel normal, we never stop to question them.

But they're not facts—they're stories. Somewhere along the way many of us picked up the belief that falling behind makes us unworthy. That doubt means we don't belong. That being unsure disqualifies us. These ideas feel personal, but they're shared. And they're wrong.

As Greene explains in *The Laws of Human Nature*, many of our deepest beliefs form long before we can challenge them. A parent who ties love to success might plant the idea that rest is laziness. A teacher who praises results over effort might convince us that our value lives in outcomes, not growth. These moments shape us. But they don't have to define us.

Imposter syndrome appears not because we're broken. It appears because we care. The more we value something, the more vulnerable it feels to step into it. That tension makes us human.

The goal isn't to silence self-doubt forever. That's impossible. It's recognizing where it came from and to stop letting it run the show. When we understand the forces that shaped these beliefs, we loosen their grip. And that's where belonging begins.

Flipping the Script

Imposter syndrome feeds on the stories we never stop to question. These invisible scripts shape how we see ourselves and what we believe we must do to belong. They sound like facts: "If I fail, I don't deserve to be here." "I have to prove I'm good enough every time I walk into the room." But they aren't facts. They're patterns, learned, repeated, and reinforced over time. These scripts don't push us to achieve as much as they shape how we think, how we speak to ourselves, and how we move through the world.

Always tying your worth to performance and believing that perfection is the only acceptable outcome is exhausting. This impossible standard has dug itself into the rich soil of our daily lives, creating the perfect environment for imposter syndrome to take root. Like an invasive species, it crowds out the native growth that makes the landscape beautiful. To become our best selves, we have to contain the invasive species and nurture the conditions in which our native selves can plant strong roots.

The roots rely on the rules, and to change those rules we must name them. Notice the moments when self-doubt rises, when you hesitate to speak, when you shrink after a mistake. Those reactions aren't random. They come from old stories that taught you that what mattered most was being right, being strong, or being impressive.

You don't have to accept those stories. You can challenge them. When the voice in your head says, "I'm not ready," ask where that voice came from. When it says, "I don't belong," ask what proof it has. Then ask what you would say to a friend who felt the same way. Most of us speak truth to others and shout fear to ourselves.

This kind of rewriting doesn't happen all at once. The old script will show up again. But each time it does, you get another chance to answer with something new. Try a different line. Try "I'm learning." Try "I showed up." Try "My value doesn't depend on perfection."

These are a new foundation. Thoughts shape behavior. Repetition shapes belief. Each time you replace the old story with something honest and strong, you build trust with yourself.

You won't silence doubt forever. But you can stop it from calling the shots. You can stop chasing proof and start standing in your place. That shift takes work. It takes patience. But most important of all, it takes awareness.

Some thoughts you carry didn't come from you. Others handed down these thoughts, passing them off as truth and never questioning them. Now you can question them. You can write something better. For me, rewriting started by realizing this: Not all my thoughts were mine. Some belonged to a place that prized stoicism over struggle, a culture that taught me to earn every breath of confidence. Recognizing that helped me separate my story from the one I inherited.

Introspection

What's one belief about success or belonging might be holding you back? How could you reframe it to help you grow?

The Power of Connection

Imposter syndrome thrives in isolation. It convinces you that your doubts are yours alone, that everyone else has it together while you're falling behind. It whispers that if you share your struggles, you'll only prove you don't belong. So you stay quiet. You fake it. The silence grows heavier.

Silence is where the lie survives. Connection is where it breaks.

When we open up about our doubts, something shifts. We hear it in someone else's voice. We see the flicker of recognition in his or her eyes. We realize we're not the only ones carrying this weight. A quiet nod, a shared story, a simple "I've felt that too" can tear a hole in the wall we thought we had to build around ourselves. That's the moment shame loses its grip.

I've felt that shift firsthand. In one of my former jobs I led advisory boards with groups of physicians involving some of the most respected clinicians and researchers in their fields. From the first meeting I felt outmatched. These doctors carried decades of experience and strung-together credentials like "Dr.," "MD," and "PhD" before and after their names. Meanwhile, I feared one wrong question would expose me as a fraud who didn't belong in the room, just another plain old guy with a boring "Mr." before his name.

A friend and colleague named Tom Tavino saw how tense I was. Before the meeting started, he pulled me aside and said, "I was nervous during my first one too. Honestly, I still get a little nervous before every ad board. But you built the content. You know how to lead this discussion. These physicians know medicine. You know how to guide the conversation. That's your job. And you're good at it."

That moment changed everything. His words didn't erase the pressure, but they gave me something stronger than confidence. They gave me clarity. I had a role. I brought value. And I wasn't alone. They didn't expect me to know everything they knew. My role was to get them talking about everything they knew. Tom reminded me of my role, preparation, and skills. That gave me the confidence to do the job at hand.

Connection doesn't solve imposter syndrome. But it gives us a different way to carry it. You don't have to face self-doubt in isolation. A friend, a mentor, a peer (someone who sees you) can help you see yourself again.

You might find connection in quiet places: a trusted conversation over coffee, a team meeting in which someone speaks the truth, a message from someone who says, "You're not the only one." These moments won't fix everything, but they shift something inside you. These moments remind you that you don't earn belonging through perfection. It's something we share.

If you want to invite more of that into your life, start where you feel most seen. Maybe it's a friend who listens without trying to fix you. Maybe it's someone you admire who's farther down the path. Or maybe it's a community of people who know what it feels like to strive, stumble, and keep going anyway.

You don't need a crowd. You need someone who knows the truth and will say it out loud.

The next time that voice in your head says, *You're the only one who feels this way*, reach out. Chances are, someone will say what you need to hear most: "I feel that way too."

Not the Stumble but the Stand

Imposter syndrome says your worth depends on getting it right. That one mistake means you're out, that everyone else has it figured out and you're still fumbling with the basics. Those ideas don't hold up. They miss what matters.

Your worth isn't found in the moments you stuck the landing. It shows up when you return after doubt, when you try again despite things going sideways, when you choose to care, to grow, to keep going.

Think back to the kid on the football field: twelve yards with a loose helmet and a shaky grip. Not flawless, not the fastest—but still running, still trying, still getting up after the hit. It wasn't the highlight because it ended in triumph. It mattered because I climbed to my feet when everything else in the world told me to stay buried in the turf.

That's the pattern—not just in games but also in life. The path forward doesn't follow a script. You won't always look polished. You won't always feel sure. Each time you keep moving, including the times with scraped knees and pockets full of doubts, you're building something stronger than certainty. You're building trust in yourself.

When the voice says you're falling short, ask what that means. Ask what really counts. A specific accomplishment of the moment may impress and leave you feeling worthy, but it is fleeting. What lasts is resilience. The choice to show up time and time again without guarantees. Success never comes with a guarantee. The world will always offer reasons to believe you're not enough. Trust yourself. Lean on genuine friends. Move forward despite all of it. Do it for yourself.

Look at your own story. Where did you keep going? Where did you stand up when it would have been easier to sit down? Those are the pages worth rereading.

This chapter doesn't end with a fix. Rather, it ends with a truth: You're already in motion. You don't need to be perfect. You don't need to outrun doubt. You do need to take the next step as yourself. Keep showing up for what matters to you.

We'll get into tools and strategies next. For now, breathe. Take a second to recognize how far you've come, even if your oversized helmet's blocking half of your vision.

CHAPTER 3

Your Brain Is Lying to You

You hit "send."

The moment the email disappears, dread rises like a wave. You scroll back and spot it: a missing word—*not*. You wrote "I am available to present this" instead of "I am *not* available to present this."

Panic grabs the mic.

Your brain leaps into action, admonishing, "You told the VP you're presenting next week. That meeting? The one in which you'll stand in front of fifty people with no slides and zero prep? You've wrecked the whole thing."

The spiral begins.

"Why didn't you double-check?" it pokes. "Why didn't you pause? Why do you have a job here?"

The soundtrack in your head changes from Miles Davis's soothing jazz masterpiece "Kind of Blue" to the Sex Pistols' anger-laden "Never Mind the Bollocks, Here's the Sex Pistols." The office disappears. Now it's a courtroom.

Exhibit A: the email.

Exhibit B: your résumé, which now reads like something from a Looney Tunes cartoon.

The prosecutor, who sounds a lot like you, shouts, "They're going to figure it out!" Your entire world is now out of control.

That's how it works.

Your brain doesn't report facts—it writes daytime soap operas. Everything becomes exaggerated. Other characters plot your downfall. Every moment leads to a new cliff-hanger. You tune in tomorrow for another episode with another failure and another cliff-hanger. It goes on like this for decades. There is never any real resolution or positive outcome.

The worst part? You believe it—because, well, it's your brain telling you these things. Why on earth would your brain ever mislead you? Worse still, the voice your brain uses sounds like you. Of course, you're going to listen. Meanwhile, it remembers only all your bad highlight reels. That time you tripped in front of the entire class. The joke that landed flat on a first date. The name you forgot before asking someone if she was pregnant (she wasn't and you still can't remember her name). And of course, the *not* you missed in today's email. Your brain loops all of it on a 4K screen with studio-quality sound until it feels like fact.

Your brain lies. Not always, but most of the time. Worse yet, when you care, it lies better than a politician.

Imposter syndrome doesn't whisper wisdom. It hijacks your mind like *The Matrix* and builds a false world in which you always fall short. It's a glitch with emotional consequences. Its goal? Keep you safe. And the safest route? Stay small. Don't risk or stretch yourself. Best not to show up. Blend in. It's the chaos DJ behind the booth, blasting a playlist called *self-doubt* every time you step onto the dance floor.

That voice doesn't scream during routine tasks. It roars when the stakes rise. When you step into something new, speak up—or risk being your authentic self.

That's when your brain pulls old files referencing outdated beliefs, shaky memories, unresolved fears. It then writes a story in which you fail.

The truth does not matter. Control is the goal.

But thoughts are inputs. Some are helpful. Some are garbage. Your job is to learn the difference. When do you need to lean in and listen? And when do you need to tell your brain to shut up?

You don't need to fight every thought. You don't need to chase them or argue with them. You do need to recognize the noise.

Your brain is loud, not accurate. The goal isn't silence—it's agency. You choose the station. That chaos DJ may pick the wrong soundtrack, but you don't have to dance to every beat.

Let's change the track.

A Day in the Life of a Liar

The mind often acts like the worst friend we've ever had. It cancels plans, gaslights us, and whispers the harshest things at the worst possible moments. It knows exactly what to say to throw us into a tailspin because it knows us better than anyone else. For me, it often starts the second I get dressed. My mind has informed me more than once that my sock choice doesn't "match" my pants and everyone will know I'm an unrefined so-and-so not worthy of being heard by anyone. Ridiculous, I know. But that's the kind of nonsense my mind feeds me. I bet yours does something similar. So let's take a look at how our brains bend the truth over the course of an ordinary day.

At Work: "I Don't Belong"

The alarm yells like a three-month-old with colic. You fall out of bed and throw on what you hope counts as professional clothing. You second-guess the shirt and jacket. Should you have ironed your pants? Now the whole outfit feels suspect. Too much pattern? Not enough competence? You haven't left your bedroom yet and you're already frustrated by your awkward place in the world.

You head out the door to a job that still feels like a stretch. In meetings you nod with intent. Someone talks about pipeline velocity and conversion metrics. You scribble notes and act as if the words land. You wonder how everyone else knows so much. Do they have access to some secret report system? Did you miss a company-wide glossary? Have you failed to read every verb in the 9,000 emails you get each week?

They speak with ease. You swim upstream.

At lunch you rehearse your update for the afternoon check-in. You revise it three times, cutting out anything that might sound unsure. When your turn comes, you speak with focus and pray that no one asks follow-ups.

They do.

Your manager leans in. "Can you walk me through your second point again?"

You pause and a split second of silence descends upon the room. He always does this—grabs onto something minor, then pulls it apart as if it holds the key to the universe. It throws you off, providing enough space for the liar in your head to take a breath.

They noticed. That pause gave you away. They're already texting HR.

You repeat your key point three times. It's solid. It matters. But it tumbles out tangled and stiff. You ramble. You lose track of your closing sentence.

Back at your desk your heart pounds. You didn't crash the meeting. You made a useful point. But your brain edits the replay and casts you as a fraud.

You're not unqualified—you're new. You're learning. But the liar rides along, whispering, *You don't belong here.*

At Home: "I'm Failing at This"

You get home determined to be there for your child. You sit down for homework time and pray that today it will go as it should. A fifteen-minute hop and skip through a couple of basic math problems.

It never does.

It's always a ninety-minute war between your child's drifting focus, your inability to grasp the ever-changing methods of elementary math, and your evaporating patience. All of it works together to defeat you as with Napoleon at Waterloo.

You ask, "Need help with math?"

Your child nods. You brace yourself.

You read the problem twice. It sounds like a riddle. Something about trains and distance and someone leaving a station at 2:15. You work through it out loud, sketching a little chart.

Your kid interrupts. "That's not how we're supposed to do it."

You ask what the teacher showed the class.

Your child shrugs. That shrug slices through the last thread of your patience.

You try again. Your child sighs. You erase and start over. Your child groans. You explain one more time. Your child throws down the pencil and says, "This is why I don't ask you."

That one lands.

You swallow the sting and walk away before you say something as reckless as what your parents said to you when you were a kid. You still carry those words. They still sting.

Later your child asks for a snack. You hand over a granola bar and stay quiet. Your child eats in silence. You scroll your phone and spot a post from another parent. The caption says, "I love seeing learning click! She begged me for extra practice tonight." The photo shows a smiling child surrounded by worksheets in a well-lit study nook that probably smells like essential oils and affirmation.

Your living room smells like athlete's foot and defeat.

The liar creeps in again: *You're failing at this. Your kid is going to suffer because of it.*

You want to argue. You want to point to the bedtime stories, the dance parties in the kitchen, the emergency poster board runs, the Target aisles covered in glitter. But your brain doesn't track effort. It counts only the sighs, the eye rolls, the moments when "I've had enough" turned into "I'm not enough."

You care. You show up. But the voice doesn't care about the showing up.

It waits for the pause.

With Others: *"Everyone Else Has It Together"*

You show up at the neighbors' house for what they called "a casual dinner." The store clerk helped you pick out a "decent" wine. So at least your wine incompetence can ride in the back seat for the night.

You step inside and immediately realize their version of casual looks like something from *Architectural Digest*.

The house smells like roasted garlic and clean wood. Not a dish in the sink. Their five-year-old greets you in Spanish and offers you a cheese cube on a bamboo skewer.

You pass the kitchen island and notice a whiteboard calendar. It's color-coded with events marked with things like "STEM night," "Soccer (away)," and "gratitude journal due."

You think about your own fridge. Right now it holds expired yogurt, a science worksheet with jelly stuck to it, and a magnet that says "Wine not?" There's dried peanut butter on the handle. Their refrigerator handle shines brighter than a Naval Academy cadet's shoes.

Dinner starts. Everyone shares his or her latest goals. One person started training for a half marathon. Another is launching a podcast. Someone else casually mentions teaching her kid mindfulness with morning affirmations.

You laugh in the right places, but your mind drifts. Your life looks different. Training for a marathon sounds about as practical as training to become the next lunar astronaut. You don't have time to listen to a podcast, let alone create one. And the most mindful conversation you had with your kid this week was an actual argument about how swallowing bubble gum won't let you blow bubbles out your butt.

You check your phone and pretend there's a reason to leave it on the table. There isn't. But you need something familiar to stare at while these highly functional creatures from another planet masquerade as your neighbors.

You try chiming in with a story about always wanting to learn piano. It lands sideways. Someone smiles, then gently changes the subject. You sip your drink. The liar steps in:

You're not like them. They figured out something you didn't. You're the uninvited guest at a party you said yes to. And piano? Really? Now they all think you're delusional.

Nobody says it out loud. They're kind. But the voice doesn't need proof. It watches you from across the table and whispers, *Everyone else has it together. You're the only one faking it.*

You stay a little longer, waiting for the precise moment when it's polite to leave. The fake laughs, the careful phrasing, the search for something relatable all wear you out.

Alone: "Who Am I to Share This?"

The house settles as the dishwasher hums along. You open the laptop or pull out the notebook or pick up the instrument—whatever aspirational hobby has captured your attention.

You sit for a moment, staring at the thing you care about. Maybe it's a song. A half-written essay. A business idea. A quick doodle on the back of a grocery list.

You work a few lines or notes. Something takes shape.

And then, right before the light of growth pushes through the far side of the tunnel, the voice shows up:

This is embarrassing. Who do you think you are? You'll never do this as well as the experts.

You stop to reread what you wrote, and shame rushes in. Everything ends up deleted. If someone found this, if someone heard this, they would laugh. They would point. They would use it as proof that you're not talented, not insightful, not worth listening to.

This isn't original, deep, or good.

You close the tab. You push the guitar aside. You tell yourself that you'll come back to it later.

But you don't.

Because that voice doesn't argue with facts. It doesn't need facts. It pokes the tender part of you that wants to be seen and says, *No one needs this. And if they did, they don't need it from you.*

You believe it because it sounds reasonable. *Who are you to create anything? Who are you to think your voice matters?*

But again, the truth lives underneath the lie.

You care—that's why it hurts. That's why it feels personal.

Because this thing you love? It's not about proving anything. It's about showing up. Trying. Reaching for something that feels true. And the louder the liar gets, the more it probably means you've touched something that matters.

You don't need to be perfect.

You need to keep going.

But tonight you close the laptop and go to bed with the lie still echoing in your chest:

Who am I to share this?

Doubt changes costumes, but it's still the same voice. It wears a different outfit in every room. At work it looks like inadequacy. At home it looks like failure. Around others it looks like comparison. When you're alone it looks like self-censorship. But it's the same voice. It doesn't just doubt what you do—it also questions who you are. And once you spot the pattern, you realize:

It's not telling the truth.

It's good at impressions

The Lie behind the Lies

Every doubt has a bothersome neighbor. He's loud, never knocks, kicks the door open, and starts offering his unsolicited opinion as if he owns the place. You know him. He shows up mid-thought with classics like "You're not smart enough," "You're failing at this," or "They're going to figure you out." His voice feels familiar. Confident. Persuasive. Like a walking infomercial for your worst-case scenarios.

His favorite headline?

"You're not enough."

That's the lie behind the lies. It hides beneath the surface, wearing a dozen different disguises. Sometimes it dresses up as perfectionism or procrastination. Sometimes it critiques your parenting, your résumé, your relationships, your tone of voice in a meeting. But no matter how it shows up, it always loops back to the same fear. This isn't a passing thought—it's a recurring character in your mental sitcom (more Kramer than Mr. Rogers) barging in with wild energy, emptying your fridge, and delivering unsolicited commentary on how your life is coming apart.

Here's the twist: You don't spiral over things that don't hold weight.

You don't lose sleep over a burned toaster waffle. You don't obsess about how you worded a grocery list. But send a typo to the VP? Freeze during a panel discussion? Miss your kid's game because of a deadline? Then your inner neighbor yells through the walls—because those moments hit something deeper.

They mean something to you.

That's what no one tells you. The voice gets loud in the places where you're most alive—where your values live, where you're investing your energy, your focus, your effort. Doubt doesn't linger where you're coasting. It pitches a tent at the edge of your growth, then critiques your form like an over-caffeinated gymnastics judge.

The liar didn't show up out of nowhere. Early criticism, old stories, and unspoken expectations trained it. Somewhere along the way, fear got dressed up as protection. The voice learned to scan for threats, not truth. It feels like a warning sign. But more often it's a spotlight. It shines on the moments when you're stretching, taking a risk, doing something that reflects the version of yourself you're trying to become. When you're exposed like that, the stakes feel higher. So the noise gets louder.

That doesn't make it true.

The next time your brain replays a highlight reel of every misstep from sixth grade to this morning's awkward silence, don't ask, "What's wrong with me?" Ask, "Why does this matter to me?"

The answer to that question is gold. It tells you where your heart is. Where your momentum lives. Where your story is growing.

Yes, the uninvited neighbor will keep barging in. He'll question your worth, mock your progress, and act as if he knows the ending. But he doesn't. He shows up only when you're onto something.

You're building something real, trying when it feels shaky, still standing in the arena, choosing effort over retreat.

That messy, imperfect, fully human effort? It's enough.

The "I Got Lucky" Trap

Let's talk about one of the slickest lies your brain tells. Sure, it's already busy whispering that you don't belong or that your failures define you. But *this* lie? It's sneakier. More flattering in disguise. It shows up right when something *good* happens, when you finally accomplish something meaningful and mutters, "That was nothing but luck."

Forget talent. Never mind effort. All those late nights, early mornings, and months of hard work? Irrelevant. According to your lying mind, the outcome had nothing to do with you—it was simply dumb luck.

For years I believed that about one of my biggest career milestones. During the launch year of a medicine that changed the lives of patients with a rare and deadly disease, I hit the company's top sales numbers. I should have felt proud. Instead, I told myself (and anyone who would listen) that it was because of my cross-functional teammates, a couple of high-prescribing physicians, a soft forecast, and a product that sold itself. Anything to avoid saying, "I did this."

People congratulated me and I distanced myself from the accolades as if they were a pandemic. "Right place, right time," I would say with a shrug. "Got lucky, I guess." I acted as though I had tripped over a scratch-off ticket in a parking lot and won a jackpot by accident.

Never mind the time I had spent learning each customer's mindset, digging into clinical studies, or living in hotel rooms to be present at the right moment. I didn't mention that I inherited an underdeveloped territory and had to build it one conversation at a time: finding, educating, and encouraging healthcare providers to treat the patients right in front of them.

None of that counted—not when the "luck" story offered a faster exit from discomfort.

The "I got lucky" lie doesn't feel like sabotage—it feels polite. Modest and virtuous. And I value humility. I hate arrogance. I don't want to be the guy who brags. So I downplayed it. I assumed people would *know* how hard I had worked. I was wrong. When you say something enough times, you *believe* it. And so do they.

Downplaying your success not only diminishes how you see yourself. It also trains others to do the same.

It's easier to pretend your wins were accidents than to face the awkward truth: you earned it. And if you earned it, maybe you're talented. Maybe you *deserve* the praise. But if you let that in, if you accept it, you might look like the other egomaniacs always *needing* the spotlight. Nobody wants to be *that guy*. So you feed the lie. And the lie grows legs.

I once asked a brilliant songwriter about a song of hers that went viral. It was personal, raw, unforgettable. She shrugged and said, "I got lucky. Right person shared it." But I had watched her writing, revising, playing in empty rooms for years. That moment of success hadn't fallen from the sky. It had grown from a mountain of quiet effort.

Maybe luck opened the door—but she had built the house.

Here's your reminder. Luck has a role, sure. But it doesn't write the story. *You* do. Every time you show up, do the work, stick with the process, and share something real, you're doing the part that matters.

This wasn't luck. You did the work, stayed with it, and made it happen.

When the Voice Gets Mean

Imposter syndrome often starts as background noise. You hear a flicker of doubt and push past it by staying busy and shaking it off. Most days you keep going. Then the voice changes.

The tone sharpens. The volume rises. It stops critiquing your work and aims straight at who you are. No longer "That didn't go well." Now it's "You don't belong here." Instead of "You stumbled. Now it's "you always fail." The message digs in and claims new ground.

The voice names you.

Adele, yes *that* Adele, knows that voice. One of the most celebrated artists of our time, she built a career on sold-out tours, shattered records, and that once-in-a-generation voice. Still, before big performances she suffers, as many of us suffer. She has thrown up backstage, canceled shows out of fear—not from fear of missing a note but from fear of being exposed. She once admitted, "I'm scared of audiences. At one show in Amsterdam I was so nervous that I escaped out the fire exit."

That moment says everything. A woman beloved across the globe, with talent, presence, and power, ran for the nearest door because self-doubt shouted more loudly than any crowd.

I've never dodged a concert, but I've had moments that made me want to disappear. I've stood behind microphones or in front of executives while my confidence unraveled one sentence at a time. The voice in my head didn't ask helpful questions but instead launched a full-scale identity crisis. One shaky pause and it declared me unfit, exposed, finished.

That kind of doubt doesn't whisper insecurity. It rewrites the story. You're no longer someone who had a bad day. You become the weak link, the imposter who slipped through the cracks and finally got caught.

Once the voice redefines the story, behavior shifts. The instinct becomes retreat. Hands stay down. Thoughts stay quiet. Risk shrinks. Rejection gets rehearsed before anyone else offers it.

Not everyone retreats. Some go in the opposite direction. Overcompensation kicks in. The smile stays fixed. The pace stays quick. Hands stay steady while the mind spins. Action masks fear. Everything on the outside stays composed. Inside tells a different story, a story held together by grit, not grounding. They refuse to ask for help.

Their minds tell them, *Asking for help is a weakness, a sign that you're incapable or unworthy of handling life's challenges.* It convinces us that true success comes only from doing everything on our own. But refusing to ask for help doesn't strengthen you—it makes life harder.

Think about the iconic Black Knight scene from *Monty Python and the Holy*

Grail. In a duel the knight loses an arm but refuses to acknowledge it, brushing it off with, "'Tis but a scratch!" As the fight continues he loses his other arm, then both legs. Yet he still insists he's fine while rolling around limbless and challenging his opponent to keep fighting. His sheer stubbornness is hilarious on screen. In real life, when we refuse help as we metaphorically lose all our limbs, the results aren't as funny.

For years I played the Black Knight. Juggling work, college, and raising a family, I convinced myself that asking for help meant admitting failure. Instead of leaning on friends for childcare, I brought my young son to study sessions, getting less done and exhausting us both. At work I rejected guidance from colleagues, determined to "figure it out myself," only to slow my progress. I was overcompensating for a long list of insecurities. As with the Black Knight, I kept insisting I was fine. Meanwhile, life kept hacking off limbs.

The reality? Asking for help isn't a sign of weakness—it's a mark of strength. The most successful people surround themselves with mentors, collaborators, and supporters. Athletes, no matter how talented they are, rely on coaches, trainers, and teammates to reach their full potential. Yet somehow many of us buy into the myth that we should do everything alone. But as noted before, refusing help doesn't strengthen us—it makes life harder.

When I let go of the lie and started asking for help, everything changed. Mentors offered wisdom that helped me avoid costly mistakes. Friends and colleagues stepped in when I felt overwhelmed, turning daunting tasks into manageable ones. Most importantly, I stopped isolating myself.

It is all ironic because people *want* to help. When you ask for support, you're not imposing. You're inviting connection. You're showing trust, which strengthens relationships.

The next time you hear the voice saying, "You should handle this alone," remember the Black Knight. Don't let stubbornness leave you stuck. Reaching out for help isn't a failure—it's the first step toward growth, collaboration, and resilience.

You're not stuck in the wrong battle. That voice doesn't get to name you. It doesn't get to write your story.

That voice doesn't deserve the mic anymore. It's time to name what's really happening inside your head.

Self 1 and Self 2

By now you've probably learned to recognize when the voice in your head turns from irritating to ruthless. But what you might not know is the voice isn't the entire story. It's one character in the cast.

Timothy Gallwey in his brilliant book *The Inner Game of Tennis* gives names to the two principal players inside our heads. Self 1 is the loud one. The overthinker. The running commentary that critiques, corrects, and questions every move. It's the voice that pipes up mid-sentence and says, "That sounded dumb," or rewinds an interaction from last Tuesday to point out exactly how you should have responded instead. Self 2 doesn't make a scene. This part of you already knows what to do. It remembers what you've practiced without needing commentary.

Self 2 shows up when you're not trying to impress or be perfect. It's behind the wheel when you're driving home and barely thinking about your turns. When you play that piece of music you have mastered, it ensures your fingers hit all the right notes at the exact right moment. It's there when you connect with someone, not because you rehearsed it but because you meant it. Self 2 thrives when you stop hovering over your own performance and simply let yourself be in it.

Self 2 isn't only instinct. You can train it. Every time you practice without perfectionism, show up without a script, or recover instead of spiral, you strengthen it. Self 2 isn't some mystical force you either have or don't. It gets stronger every time you practice without performance pressure, recover from a mistake without judgment, or trust your instincts instead of overthinking. This isn't magic—it's training. It grows through repetition, reflection, and trust—not in flawless execution but in the process itself. It doesn't need praise to keep going. It needs permission.

The goal isn't to silence Self 1 completely. That's not possible. And honestly, it's unnecessary. Self 1 can be useful in the right context. It knows how to plan, prepare, and rehearse. It can help you troubleshoot a presentation or organize your thoughts before a hard conversation. The problem is when Self 1 refuses to sit down once the show starts. It grabs the mic during your pitch, your performance, your parenting moment, and insists on narrating every beat while you're trying to live it.

For a long time I didn't know these two voices had names. I considered my voice broken; it was too anxious, too critical, and too loud at the worst moments. But once I learned about Gallwey's framing, something shifted. I stopped thinking I had to get rid of that inner critic and started thinking about how to stop giving it the steering wheel.

One of the biggest changes came when I started practicing what Gallwey calls "nonjudgmental awareness." That means noticing what happened without immediately assigning it a grade. I would walk out of a meeting and instead of spiraling into "That was terrible," I would say, "I stumbled at the beginning but I found my rhythm." I could observe what had happened without turning it into a character assessment.

And when I caught myself drifting into past failures or future catastrophes, I tried to go back to the moment I was actually in. That meant paying attention to something simple and real: the feeling of my feet on the floor, the sound of a colleague's voice, the breath I hadn't realized I had been holding. Self 1 loves to travel to places you've already been and to places where everything might go wrong. Self 2? Self 2 lives only in the present. You find it by coming back to *now*.

Letting go of perfection was harder. I had grown up believing that anything short of flawless was a failure. Self 1 thrived on that belief. It used every stumble as evidence that I didn't belong. Perfection is not the ticket to belonging—it's the cage.

Over time, mistakes looked less like proof of failure and more like part of the process. Not because failure suddenly felt fun, but because something shifted when I gave myself a little grace, that ever-so-precious gift I was so good at extending to other people when they made mistakes. I never stopped to consider I needed to treat myself with the same kindness I gave others. Being kind to myself and dropping the demand for perfection made space for progress. Tension eased. Connection returned. The part of me that already knew what to do, Self 2, finally had room in which to work.

One particular moment stays with me. I was preparing to speak to a large audience, the first time since learning about these two inner voices. The nerves showed up early, and of course, so did Self 1: "Don't screw this up." But instead of fighting back or pretending I was fine, I acknowledged the noise and quietly stepped aside. A deep breath. Eye contact with someone in the front row. The first sentence—delivered like a conversation, not a performance. That's when Self 2 arrived: not summoned but ready. It had been there all along, waiting for a little room.

This wasn't magic. It was practice. A different practice. The kind in which you stop trying to be perfect and start trusting that you already know more than you think. The kind in which you notice the noise without letting it control the volume, in which you give space to the part of yourself that doesn't need constant correction to perform well.

Gallwey's book taught me something I wish we had all learned earlier: confidence doesn't come from silencing every doubt. Rather, it comes from learning *which voice to trust.*

Self 1 will always be there, clipboard in hand. But it doesn't need to drive. Let it help you plan—then invite it to take a seat. When the moment comes to act, speak, create, or connect, let Self 2 take the lead.

That's the version of you that already knows what to do. It needs you to get out of the way, though.

Introspection

Where does Self 1 get loud in your life?
When was a time you acted with instinct and it worked?

Why Your Inner Critic Gets Loud When You're on the Right Track

Imposter syndrome doesn't sound the alarm when you coast. It doesn't care about the safe zones or the tasks you can do with your eyes closed. It doesn't show up during small talk or during spreadsheets you've already mastered. No, it saves its commentary for the moments that matter. It pipes up when the room gets quiet, when your name sits on the meeting agenda, when your kid looks to you for help, when you write the thing that feels a little too honest. It waits for the moments that require heart. Then it jumps onto the stage as if it owns the place.

That voice isn't a sign that something's wrong—it's a sign that something *matters*.

Your inner critic doesn't scream because you've failed—it screams because you've *entered the arena*. The one that asks for your effort, your attention, your presence. That voice gets louder as the stakes rise, which means the volume isn't the problem—it's the evidence.

Your mind wants to protect you. Self 1 loves control. It plans, scripts, critiques, and calculates. It hates risk. When you move toward something real, something unscripted, it panics. It doesn't want the mess. It wants a guarantee.

But life doesn't hand those out. So Self 1 yells. It grabs the mic and starts narrating your doom. You freeze, second-guess, and sometimes retreat. Not because the voice told the truth but because it was fast, loud, and familiar.

That voice? It never had fresh material. It loops the same tired tracks on an old playlist. The chaos DJ spinning panic beats. A stubborn Black Knight who's lost all his limbs pretending that nothing's wrong. The ghostwriter behind every worst-case scenario you've imagined.

Volume doesn't equal truth.

You showed up and stayed. You chose to stretch instead of shrink. You took the risk, tried again. You cared enough to lean into discomfort because something on the other side matters.

That's not a fraud. That's a fighter.

And that quieter presence inside you, Self 2, already knows the way.

No shouting. No spotlight. Just calm presence. It emerges when you stop performing and start connecting. It draws from your experience, your effort, your instincts. It keeps you grounded in the only place growth happens: right here, in the present, now.

The doubt doesn't mean you don't belong. Fear doesn't mean you're failing.

It all points to the same thing: *You care.*

And you don't lie to people you care about.

Stop lying to yourself.

You're not pretending. You're taking part. Work, learning, and growth are all part of your journey. And the voice that tries to tear you down? It shows up only when you're building something worth protecting.

You don't need to silence it. Don't hand it the mic, though.

That space belongs to Self 2.

And Self 2 is ready.

But when Self 2 steps in, the work isn't done. The voice might quiet, but the patterns it left behind often stay loud. One of the most persistent? Perfectionism—the armor we reach for after imposter syndrome sits down. It tells us, "If you can't silence the doubt, at least leave no room for mistakes." That armor might look like protection, but over time it weighs more than it shields. Eventually it costs more than it saves.

PART TWO

CONFRONTING
IMPOSTER SYNDROME

CHAPTER 4

Perfectionism: The Hustle that Never Ends

In the last chapter we called out the lies our minds love to tell, the whispers that say we're not enough, that we don't belong. When we believe those lies, something sneaks in and tightens its grip.

That something is perfectionism.

Perfectionism looks helpful on the surface. It acts like a motivator. It tells us to aim higher, work harder, and never let a flaw slip by. But it doesn't push us toward growth—it traps us in fear.

It's like that friend who organizes his or her sock drawer by brand of sock, then wonders why he or she can't sleep. One minute you're tidying a drawer; the next you're organizing every article of clothing by color and season, planning every outfit you will wear for the next month, and creating a shopping list to fill the gaps. You call it "attention to detail," but deep down, it's panic wearing a name tag saying, "I'm in control."

At first, perfectionism feels like ambition. But under the surface it pushes a lie. If you don't do it without any flaws, don't do it at all. That belief pulls us into two extremes: avoid everything or overdo everything.

Let's say you have a week to write a report. Easy. But the teacher returned your last report edited in red ink, each mark somehow revealing your imagined incompetence. So this one feels heavier. You stall. You convince yourself that tomorrow you'll feel ready. But as *Annie* reminds us, tomorrow is always a day away. Before you know it, it's the night before the deadline. You rush to finish, the way you crammed in high school or college. This isn't a new pattern. You don't love your finished product. But it's too late.

Or maybe you go the other way. You dive in and push hard. You fix every sentence, adjust every chart, and chase every detail. This obsession lasts for days. It's all you can think of. Everything else in your life takes a back seat to this rather inconsequential (in the grand scheme of things) assignment that you have built up to be the defining moment of your entire life. Hours fly by. It's 2 a.m. the night before it's due and your eyes burn. You don't feel done or proud. Worn out and worried are your only emotions left.

Sound familiar? That's the trap of perfectionism. It convinces us we're only as good as our latest accomplishment. It turns minor setbacks into catastrophes, stealing joy from our successes and leaving us exhausted, anxious, and unfulfilled.

This chapter unpacks the roots of perfectionism, its impact, and how to break free. Along the way we'll examine the cultural and personal forces of childhood expectations to societal pressures that fuel it. I'll equip you with practical tools to trade perfectionism for progress, helping you reclaim your energy, confidence, and creativity.

Perfection is an illusion. Chasing it can inspire growth, but holding yourself to its impossible standards only keeps you small. It's time to let go of perfectionism's grip and embrace the messy, meaningful process of growth. If perfectionism thrives on fear and impossible standards, where do those beliefs begin? To understand how it takes root in our lives, we need to trace it back to its origins.

Where the Madness Begins: How Perfectionism Gets Planted

Perfectionism doesn't show up like a winning lottery ticket at the corner store. It grows like weeds: quiet, persistent, and rooted deeply in what we live through and what we learn to expect from ourselves. Childhood, culture, and personal pain all feed it. To pull it up by the roots, we first must understand where it begins.

Perfectionism often takes root in childhood, shaped by the environments we grow up in and the messages we absorb about success and self-worth. School teaches us early that achievement matters. Results matter. A perfect test score earns a gold star. High performance gets praise. And that's not wrong. Outcomes deserve recognition and, when warranted, condemnation. But somewhere along the way, many kids believe that *only* the outcome counts, that worth hinges not on growth or effort but on the grade, the trophy, or the win.

Well-meaning adults say things like "Do your best," but many kids hear "*Be* the best." Over time the desire to improve turns into fear—a fear of falling short, a fear of disappointing someone, a fear of not measuring up. Mistakes stop being part of the process and start looking like evidence you don't belong.

That's when motivation mutates. Perfectionism stops being about striving and starts being about survival. You either hit the mark or you hide. You either deliver the win or you risk being dismissed.

In that kind of mindset, the "how" matters less than the "what." When the outcome is everything, corners get cut. Rules get bent. People cheat, manipulate, and step on others to get the win they've been taught to chase. The pressure to prove your worth can override integrity.

This early conditioning doesn't stay in the classroom. It shows up at work, in relationships, and in our own internal narratives. When approval feels tied to performance, perfectionism becomes less of a drive to grow and more of a defense against being exposed. Sometimes that defense turns ruthless.

Filtered Lives and Workplace Lies

While childhood plants the seed, culture pours on the fertilizer. We live in a world that celebrates achievement and treats failure like weakness. Social media turns up the pressure, serving an endless loop of highlight reels: perfect vacations, dream jobs, flawless families. Nobody posts the breakdowns, the doubts, the stretch marks of trying.

Culture rewards the outcome, not the process. It praises striving but hides the struggle. That creates a warped sense of reality, a world in which everyone else seems to have it all figured out. The truth gets polished like a shiny used car with a failing engine. It looks great on the outside, but it doesn't run right. Meanwhile, every person you know, every face you scroll past, is struggling with something. You are not alone. You never were.

Then there's the workplace. Perfectionism thrives in performance reviews, deadline chases, and productivity metrics. The message is loud and clear: produce, impress, repeat. Your value becomes something you measure in deliverables and flawless execution.

The pressure doesn't stay at the office. We carry it home. We carry it into our relationships, our goals, our sleep. Perfectionism climbs on your back like a weighted pack. You keep hiking, hoping nobody notices how much it hurts.

When the system values only the finish line, people stop asking if they crossed it the right way. They need to cross it first, often at the expense of everything else in their lives.

For many, perfectionism becomes a coping mechanism, a shield against criticism or judgment. If I'm perfect, no one can fault me. If I don't try, I can't fail. It's born from the fear of letting others down, the fear of being seen as less than, the fear of being exposed. Your mind convinces you that being called a failure is the worst thing that could ever happen to you.

Mistakes Were Made (and I Thought I Was One of Them)

I can still feel the knot in my stomach from report card day in middle school. My dad wasn't unreasonable, but he had expectations. A 52 percent in math didn't meet them. His frustration boiled over into red-faced, angry yelling.

Desperate to ease the tension, I cracked a joke: "Well, I got half of it right." He didn't laugh.

That moment stuck—not because he was wrong to want more from me but because I internalized a message he never meant to send. He didn't say *I* wasn't enough. However, that's what I heard. His reaction taught me that mistakes weren't mistakes—they were evidence I was a failure. Worse still, that failure was mine to fix alone.

His yelling didn't push me to improve. It made me afraid of him. Never mind that I struggled with the material. Never mind that I lacked the focus and structure I needed to sit down and learn. His reaction, like that of thousands of other well-meaning parents, didn't invite me to ask for help. It told me to hide, to deal with it on my own.

From that point on, perfectionism dug in. As a kid I procrastinated not because I was lazy but from fear. I left assignments untouched because of feeling overwhelmed. What if it wasn't good enough? What if it proved I couldn't do it? If I waited until the last minute, I could blame the clock instead of my ability—I "ran out of time."

As an adult, that same fear didn't lead to procrastination—it led to overwork. Instead of avoiding the tasks, I obsessed over them. I stayed late after everyone else had gone home. I spent Saturday mornings "keeping caught up," convinced that if I didn't stay ahead, I would fall behind. The more I achieved, the more I felt pressure to prove I deserved it. No amount of effort ever silenced the voice that whispered, *If you stop, you'll fail.*

Perfectionism Is a Liar (but a Convincing One)

The roots of perfectionism run deeply by twisting through childhood messages, cultural pressures, and personal fear. We learn early on that our value seems to depend on how well we perform. Once that belief takes hold, it's hard to shake. What starts as motivation becomes a survival strategy. Perfectionism is about protection. It's a shield we use to avoid feeling exposed or not enough.

Recognizing that truth is the first step. When we see perfectionism not as a strength but as a fear response, we loosen its grip. This isn't about giving up on success—it's about changing what success means.

Awareness isn't enough. Knowing the roots helps, but it doesn't undo the damage. The actual work begins when we face the toll perfectionism takes: the burnout, the anxiety, the missed moments, the relationships strained under the weight of trying to hold it all together.

Perfectionism always demands a price. The longer we chase it, the more it costs.

The Hustle Tax: What Perfectionism Takes from You

Perfectionism often disguises itself as a virtue, a relentless drive for excellence, a commitment to the highest standards. But beneath its polished surface, perfectionism wreaks havoc. It seeps into every corner of our lives, draining our energy, straining our relationships, and leaving us dissatisfied.

What makes perfectionism insidious is its dual nature. For some it manifests as procrastination, a fear of starting anything that might fall short of impossible standards. For others it drives workaholism, a relentless pursuit of doing more, being more, achieving more, all to quiet the voice that whispers, *You're not enough.* Let's look at the "hustle tax" in action and how perfectionism charges interest on your energy, time, and peace of mind.

Procrastination: When Doing the Dishes Feels like Destiny

Procrastination is perfectionism's favorite disguise. It whispers, *Why start if it won't be perfect?* It convinces us to delay while we alphabetize our spice rack or reorganize our inbox. Sure—procrastination loves to masquerade as productivity, but beneath the tidy inbox lies fear of starting, failing, or being seen as less than enough. It's not just avoidance—it's self-preservation, an attempt to shield ourselves from the discomfort of imperfection.

The irony? This hesitation often leads to rushed, subpar results—the very outcome perfectionists dread. Meanwhile, tasks pile up, deadlines loom, and anxiety mounts, like a bad sitcom in which the main character keeps digging himself or herself into a bigger hole. Except this time *you're* both the star and the audience cringing from the sidelines.

As a kid I knew this game well. Homework sat untouched while I lost myself in video games or pickup football. If I put off starting, then failure wasn't about ability—it was poor time management.

Workaholism: Where Lunch Breaks Go to Die

While some perfectionists freeze, others sprint. Workaholism is procrastination's overachieving twin—the one who wakes up at 5 a.m., schedules back-to-back meetings, and wears *busyness* like a badge of honor. At first glance, workaholics seem like the model of success. They stay late at the office, take on extra projects, and scoff at the idea of lunch breaks. It feels noble and necessary. But behind the color-coded calendars and 70-hour workweeks is a deeper fear: *If I stop for a moment, the illusion of control will shatter.*

This was me. If childhood was about avoiding failure, adulthood became a race to outrun it. Busyness became my default, and I piled on responsibilities until I felt buried. Saying yes to everything seemed like the only way to prove my worth. I volunteered for every extra project. I stayed late while my coworkers disappeared at 5:01 p.m. (*Where did they go? Did they know something I didn't?*) I convinced myself that pushing harder would keep imposter syndrome at bay. If I worked a little more, got one more thing right, maybe I would feel that I belonged.

But I didn't. Instead, I burned myself out. I sacrificed sleep, time with family, and any concept of "free time"—all in the name of proving I was enough. My idea of "relaxing" became answering emails in sweatpants. Vacations? A great time to catch up on work!

Here's what I didn't see then: Workaholism is creativity's worst enemy. When you're sprinting to stay ahead, there's no room to wonder, to explore, to play. You don't take creative risks when your brain's stuck in survival mode. Playing it safe is your only mode. Stick to what you know because you're too busy double-checking your sixth revision of a PowerPoint slide to ask, *What if we tried something different?*

Perfectionism whispers that innovation is dangerous and that different might be wrong. Wrong might be fatal. So we stay in the lines. Beautiful coloring, but only in blue.

The irony? Procrastination and workaholism cannot provide relief. One avoids discomfort; the other sinks under it. Both grow from the same fear: the belief that unless we do everything perfectly, others will see us as unworthy. That fear distorts the truth.

Burnout: Congratulations. You Played Yourself

Perfectionism promises success, but more often it delivers a slow-motion meltdown. It whispers that your self-worth depends on flawless execution, that rest is laziness, and that the smallest misstep is a neon sign screaming *inadequate.* Whether it shows up as procrastination or workaholism, the result is the same: You run yourself into the ground. When the crash comes, it's called burnout.

Burnout isn't about being tired. It's about being disconnected from your creativity, your joy, and sometimes from yourself. Burnout feels like Netflix pausing the series marathon and asking, *Are you still watching?* Then you realize: Not really. You're zoning out to yet another soap opera dressed up in a medieval power struggle with flying dragons, too tired to carry yourself to the bedroom and mad that pizza isn't the healthiest food you could ever eat.

The worst part? You never see it coming, especially if you're a perfectionist. The very work that once lit you up feels suffocating. You dread what you used to enjoy. Hobbies gather dust. Relationships become strained. You believe that if you could push a little harder, get one more thing right, or squeeze in one more win, the emptiness might lift. Spoiler: *It won't.*

Burnout feeds off the same fear that fuels the classic perfectionist trap of the all-or-nothing mindset. Miss one workout, and now you eat an entire cake for dinner. Forget a meeting, and now they're going to fire you. Snap at a friend, and now you're the villain in everyone's story. This is the logic of a perfectionist: One wrong note ruins the whole song.

That thinking? It's like abandoning your car because it's out of gas. A single slip doesn't erase your progress—it makes you human. As jazz great Miles Davis once said, "It's not the note you play that's wrong—it's the note you play afterward that makes it right." Mistakes are part of how music finds its shape.

But when you're in it, all the way in it, perfectionism insists there's only one way out: to try harder. So you do. The hustle ramps up. Emails get answered from bed. "Relaxing" looks like catching up on work. Every open space on the calendar gets filled, as if the right combination of effort and efficiency might chase the dread away. It doesn't. Because the actual answer isn't more effort—it's more grace.

Breaking free from burnout and all-or-nothing thinking doesn't mean abandoning ambition. Success isn't about flawless execution; it's about learning to keep going when the path gets messy. Progress matters more than perfection, and showing up with blemishes keeps us moving forward—because no one is handing out trophies for being the most exhausted. No one's writing a song about the person who answered Slack messages at midnight while eating cold pizza in pajama pants.

What matters isn't a perfect performance. It's how consistently you show up. Imperfect, yes. But present and still in the game.

Relationships: When You Expect Mind-Reading and Get the Wrong Coffee

Perfectionism affects not only how we work but also how we connect with others. When we hold ourselves to impossible standards, we often impose those same expectations on the people around us. We expect our partners, friends, or colleagues to anticipate our needs, respond flawlessly, or meet our unspoken ideals.

A friend of mine once described her marriage as "death by a thousand disappointments." She expected her husband to know what to say during every disagreement, to make grand romantic gestures without being asked, and to anticipate her needs like a mind-reading golden retriever. When he fell short, as we all do, she took it as a lack of care. Resentment built one quiet unmet need after another until neither of them knew how to name it.

And look—as a man I can confirm: We're going to fall short. I told my daughter that when she was ten. She had made a face after a group of boys at school did something gross, and I nodded and said, "Boys are gross."

Her hopeful eyes looked at me and replied, "But Daddy—*you're* a boy."

"Yes," I said, "but go ask your mommy if I'm gross." She did. Mommy confirmed.

We're all flawed, some of us in more obvious ways than others. And when you expect perfection from the people around you, things get messy fast. You end up annoyed that your friend didn't telepathically know you needed a pick-me-up coffee, or irritated that your partner loaded the dishwasher "wrong," as if there's a scientific method for loading plates and bowls and your partner committed a dishwasher felony.

Perfectionism also makes vulnerability feel like a risk. When we're obsessed with maintaining a flawless image, we hesitate to share our struggles or insecurities. This reluctance to be real can prevent deep, meaningful connections.

The Hustle Tax: What Perfectionism Costs You

Whether it takes the form of procrastination, overwork, or high expectations for others, perfectionism grows out of the fear of falling short. It traps us in a cycle of stress, avoidance, and doubt. It tells us that only flawless performance can earn us value. The cost runs deep. It drains our time, energy, and joy. It damages relationships, harms our health, and stifles our potential. Still, many of us hold on, believing that if we work harder, we will feel that we measure up.

But worth does not come from constant achievement. We already have it. Letting go of perfectionism does not mean lowering the bar. It means changing what we aim for: choosing growth, connection, and self-respect over impossible standards.

To change course, we need first to see where those standards come from. We did not invent them—we absorbed them. From childhood cartoons to classic novels to the way history tells its favorite stories, we have learned that success means perfection and anything less means failure.

The Cultural Mirror: How Our Favorite Characters Got Us Here

Personal struggles do not encompass the entirety of perfectionism. It shows up in the stories we tell about ourselves, our heroes, and what it means to succeed. From cartoon characters to literary icons to real-world legends, the pursuit of perfection drives achievement but often leads to burnout, disconnection, or collapse.

For a lighthearted glimpse into the absurdity of perfectionism, look no further than *SpongeBob SquarePants*. In one memorable episode, SpongeBob enters a competitive bubble-blowing contest against his longtime rival, Squidward. Determined to create the perfect bubble, he doesn't just inflate it— he polishes it, inspects it from every angle, and protects it from nonexistent threats, all while Squidward rolls his eyes. SpongeBob's obsession grows so intense that he refuses to celebrate, breathe too hard, or move. He's terrified that something, anything, might ruin his masterpiece.

Of course, despite all his efforts, the inevitable happens. The bubble pops. Because, well—that's what bubbles do.

SpongeBob's relentless pursuit of perfection captures the essence of real-world perfectionism. The harder we try to control every detail, the more we set ourselves up for frustration. As with SpongeBob's bubble, perfection is always fragile. One misstep, one uncontrollable factor, and it pops.

This mirrors real life. Think about a young artist erasing and redrawing the same lines, terrified of sharing his or her work until it's "perfect." Or the professional who revises a presentation so many times that he or she loses sight of its purpose. The pursuit of perfection often leads to exhaustion, missed opportunities, and a lot of unnecessary stress.

I get it and still do it from time to time. I've edited this book at least seven times and still feel that it needs more work. At this rate I might keep editing forever, chasing some mythical "perfect" version that doesn't exist. Meanwhile, the bubble I've been protecting, my supposed masterpiece, threatens to pop under the weight of my own expectations.

F. Scott Fitzgerald's *The Great Gatsby* offers a more sobering perspective on perfectionism. Jay Gatsby's life is a relentless pursuit of an unattainable ideal, reclaiming Daisy Buchanan, his lost love. To achieve this, Gatsby reinvents himself, transforming from a poor farm boy into a wealthy enigma. His lavish parties, sprawling mansion, and curated image all serve one goal: proving his worthiness to Daisy.

But the person Gatsby idealizes doesn't exist. She's a projection of his own fantasies, and his obsession with perfection blinds him to reality. In chasing an unattainable dream, Gatsby sacrifices authenticity and meaningful connections. In the end, his perfectionism leads to his downfall. His dream shatters, and so does he.

Gatsby's story resonates with anyone who's ever felt that happiness lies beyond his or her reach. Perfectionism convinces us we're one step away from "enough." If only we could land that promotion, lose those ten pounds, or master that skill. The constant striving disconnects us from the present and leaves us chasing shadows.

In world history few figures embody perfectionism's double-edged sword as Alexander the Great. By age thirty he had conquered much of the known world, building an empire that stretched from Greece to India. His ambition was unmatched. He sought not only victory but also absolute domination, demanding excellence from himself and unwavering loyalty from his troops.

His relentless pursuit of greatness came at a cost. The Macedonian army, exhausted after years of nonstop campaigning, refused to march any farther. His closest allies grew wary of his insatiable need for conquest. Unwilling to accept limits, Alexander pushed forward anyway. Isolated and paranoid, he turned against those who once supported him, executing friends and generals he suspected of betrayal. At thirty-two years of age he died under mysterious circumstances, leaving behind an empire too vast to sustain and a legacy that was both awe-inspiring and tragic.

Alexander's story reminds us that while perfectionism can drive extraordinary achievement, it can also leave destruction in its wake. Ambition without balance leads to burnout, and a singular obsession with success often comes at the cost of connection, well-being, and sustainability. Conquering the world means little if you destroy yourself while doing it.

The False Promise of "Perfect"

Perfectionism shows up like a motivational speaker, all about excellence, discipline, and high standards. But give it five minutes and it turns into that friend who says he or she is "being honest" before pointing out your flaws. It doesn't make you better. It keeps you stuck. You fix one thing, then another, then another, hoping the next tweak will fill you with a sense of belonging. Spoiler: It doesn't.

What perfectionism delivers is stress, paralysis, and an unsatisfying sense that nothing you do is quite enough. You end up stuck in a loop of overthinking, overworking, and wondering why the people who seem less stressed than you are finishing things.

Perfectionism isn't about excellence—it's about fear, the fear of messing up, being judged, or not measuring up. It promises control but gives you anxiety and a half-finished project folder.

It's also an illusion. The harder we chase it, the more fragile and fleeting it becomes.

So how do we break up with it? What does it look like to stop chasing perfection and start choosing progress instead? That's what we're digging into next: with less pressure, more pizza, and no shame.

What If "Messy" Is the Point?

Mistakes carry a reputation they don't deserve. From red marks on homework to awkward silences after a misstep at work, we learn to avoid anything resembling failure. Perfectionism builds on that fear. It whispers that every mistake means something about your worth, that if you stumble it means you're not ready, not capable, not enough.

But growth comes from the stumble, not from staying still.

Think about building furniture from a certain Swedish store. The instructions confuse you. The parts all look the same. Somewhere around step four you realize the shelf faces the wrong direction. You pause. A perfectionist might feel stuck, certain that he or she has ruined it. Someone focused on progress turns the shelf around and finishes the job. It's not perfect, but it stands. It works. That's a success.

Serena Williams did not build her tennis legacy on natural talent alone. She trained for years, studied her matches, and returned to the court after losses. Her strength came from repetition and adjustment. Each mistake gave her new information to build on. That is the heart of practice.

Brené Brown, a researcher and storyteller who studies shame and vulnerability, once stood on a stage and admitted she didn't have it all together. Her talk, "The Power of Vulnerability," went viral not because she sounded flawless. Rather, it connected because she told the truth. She shared her own doubts, fears, and imperfect process. She stayed present in the discomfort. People listened because they saw themselves in her honesty. She built trust by being real.

This same shift can happen in your own life. Trying something new and struggling through it is not failure—it's evidence that you care. It's proof you're in motion. Whether you write a rough draft, speak up in a meeting, or admit you don't have the answer, you're showing up in the world instead of hiding from it.

Nothing gets better until we begin. And beginning often looks messy.

But a poor start is still a start.

Success never comes from getting it right the first time. And it never follows a straight line. The story of someone who climbs one flawless milestone after another? That's fiction. Real growth looks different. It includes progress, yes, but also plateaus, detours, and the occasional step backward. Psychologist and author Angela Duckworth, best known for her book *Grit*, calls this kind of persistence exactly that—grit, the ability to keep going when the work stops feeling exciting. Her research shows grit often predicts success more than talent or IQ. It's the long haul, consistent effort over time that matters most.

Talent alone does not predict success. It's the willingness to show up, mess up, and keep moving. That process may stretch you. It may test your patience. But it builds something stronger than perfection ever could: resilience.

Perfectionism says don't move unless it's flawless. Growth says, "Move anyway."

If you wait until you feel ready, you'll wait forever. If you move forward while unsure, you'll grow stronger every time. Messy action is not a sign of failure. It's the sign that you're becoming someone stronger than perfection ever promised.

Rest and Reboot: You're Not a Machine

Workaholism wears the mask of ambition. It convinces you that the longer you push, the more you care. It tells you to skip breaks, answer emails at midnight, and measure your worth by your output. On the outside it looks like drive. Underneath—it's fear that if you slow down you'll fall behind, that if you don't always prove your value, someone will notice.

Perfectionism feeds that fear. It promises that if you keep going, keep pushing yours and everyone else's limits, you'll reach the moment when you feel caught up, confident, and enough. But that moment never shows up. The inbox always fills, and the project list grows. The pressure resets each morning like an alarm clock you didn't ask to set.

Nature did not design your brain to run without recovery. Think of it like a smartphone. When the battery drains and the screen freezes, you don't scream at the phone. You plug it in. You let it rest. The brain works the same way. It needs time to reset. Without that space, your thoughts jam together. You forget simple things. You stare at a task for an hour and somehow make it worse. That's not failure. That's fatigue.

We live in a world that rewards nonstop motion. Hustle gets applause. Rest often gets misfiled as laziness. It's not. It's fuel. Without rest, you burn through your energy, creativity, and patience. You stop bringing your full self to your work. You become a robot with glitchy settings.

Rest does not have to be dramatic or elaborate. You don't need to spend a weekend in silence or take a sabbatical in the forest. You need a few real minutes to stop performing, to stop scrolling, to let your brain do something that feels like nothing.

Put on a song you loved in high school. Watch a video of a cat who runs the household. Go outside and stare at a tree. Take a nap and call it a strategic mental reset. Drink water and sit still. You are not wasting time. Your mind and energy need recharging.

Creating, leading, learning, and connecting all break down without energy. And that energy doesn't come from pushing harder—it comes when you pause. Rest brings clarity. It gives your mind a chance to sort through the noise and step back from the edge. It loosens the grip of anxiety and makes room for ideas to rise.

I've lost count of the times I powered through a day in a stress fog, convinced that I was facing a mountain of impossible problems. It felt as if a thousand things were on fire. But then I slept. I woke up the next morning, and those thousand problems had become five or six. Nothing had changed except the fact that I had let myself stop.

You are not a machine. No one is handing out medals for running yourself into the ground. You don't become more valuable by ignoring your limits. True value and presence come when you take care of yourself first.

The work will still be there when you return. But you'll bring a different version of yourself, a version that remembers that life is not a sprint and that rest is not a reward—it's a requirement.

You're Not Supposed to Do It Alone

Perfectionism tries to convince us that independence is the goal. Do it on your own. Only the incapable ask for help. Cover up the messy middle. If you need support, you must not be ready. Your struggles prove you aren't capable enough.

None of that is true. Success isn't solo. And failure isn't fatal.

Take J. K. Rowling. Before Harry Potter became a global phenomenon, she faced rejection from twelve publishers. She was a single mother writing in cafés, unsure if anyone would ever care about a boy with a lightning scar. But then one publisher agreed to publish her work. And with that came edits, support, design help, and an entire team of people who believed in her work. She didn't do it alone. She wrote the story, yes. Others helped it grow. Without that collaboration, we might never have known Harry, Hermione, or Hogwarts.

Michael Jordan said, "I've failed over and over and over again in my life. And that's why I succeed." This is the same man who got cut from his high school varsity team, missed over 9,000 shots in his career, and lost 300 games. One of the greatest the game has ever seen didn't become a legend by avoiding failure. He earned his legacy by showing up again and again. Instead of folding under pressure, he looked at each mistake and asked what it could teach him. He didn't train in isolation or carry the weight alone. Coaches guided him. Teammates pushed him. Mentors challenged him. Every step of the way, support shaped his success. And he gave them credit.

Perfectionism teaches us to prove our worth through isolation and over-performance. But genuine success looks different. It includes connection, feedback, support, and a willingness to admit when you don't know the answer.

Becoming an expert isn't a requirement for asking a question. Burnout shouldn't have to come before a boundary. Rock bottom doesn't need to be the moment that grants permission to say, "I could use some help."

Progress thrives in community. Resilience grows when you realize you're not the only one who feels overwhelmed. Creativity expands when you share your ideas out loud, sometimes before they're formed. You're not supposed to have all the answers. You're not supposed to carry every burden. And you're not supposed to pretend everything's fine while falling apart.

You don't need to earn your worth through struggle. You need to remember that asking for help is not weakness. It's wisdom. It's strength. And it's beginning to build something real.

Moving beyond Perfectionism

Letting go of perfectionism doesn't mean abandoning ambition or lowering your standards. It means redefining success in a way that values progress, effort, and authenticity over impossible ideals. When we release ourselves from the grip of perfectionism, we make room for creativity, resilience, and genuine connection.

Imagine what your life could look like without perfectionism's weight. Picture yourself walking through a day without the constant need to prove your worth. Picture the freedom to take risks, knowing that mistakes won't shatter your confidence but shape it. Imagine the joy of finishing a project not because it's flawless but because it's yours: a reflection of your creativity, effort, and growth.

Think about the moments in your life when you've felt most alive or fulfilled. Were they defined by flawlessness? Probably not. Chances are, they were times when you embraced the process, took a risk, or allowed yourself to be present in the moment. Perhaps it was when you learned something new and laughed at your early attempts. Maybe it was when you shared a vulnerable truth with someone close to you and felt seen. Those moments weren't perfect but they were meaningful. That's what matters.

The irony is that perfectionism holds us back from the very things we care most about. It keeps us stuck in procrastination, with the fear of starting because we might not get it right. It stops us from sharing our work, convinced that others will judge us. It silences our voice, making us doubt whether we're good enough to speak up. When we stop chasing the illusion of perfection, we free ourselves to focus on what's real: our growth, our relationships, and our impact on the world.

The irony of perfectionism is that it promises protection but fuels the very fear we're trying to escape. Letting go of perfection doesn't erase fear. It shifts the spotlight. The actual fear underneath it all? We fear that without perfection; others will see and judge our true selves. That's where we go next. Because the actual struggle isn't only perfectionism—it's the fear that without perfectionism, others will see us as we are.

Breaking free from perfectionism isn't about abandoning your spice rack or ignoring deadlines. It's about stepping off the hamster wheel of self-doubt and realizing that life's too short to agonize over every misplaced comma or missed workout. You're not here to be perfect—you're here to be human.

Introspection

Imagine stepping into tomorrow unburdened by perfection.
What could you create? Who might you become?

CHAPTER 5

Putting Fear Back in the Box

Fear doesn't always crash into the room. It often sneaks in wearing a disguise. For me it usually shows up around 2 a.m., when I should be sleeping but instead I'm rehearsing tomorrow's meeting in my head as if it's opening night on Broadway. My brain casts fear as the director, barking orders: "Run the slides again! Double-check the data! Don't you dare let them see you stumble!" By sunrise I've already lived through six imaginary disasters all leading to my being "found out" as a fraud, none of which ever happens, of course, but all of which leave me exhausted before the day starts.

Fear is rarely subtle. Once it gets a foothold, it turns everyday worries into full-on musicals, complete with dramatic lighting and way too many costume changes. As ridiculous as those mental productions are, they reveal something important. Fear has a knack for rewriting reality when it thinks it's running the show.

If chapter 4 taught us anything, it's that perfectionism is sneaky. It convinces us that if we try hard enough, prepare long enough, and never mess up, we'll be safe. There's a catch-22 of sorts: The more tightly we cling to perfection, the more terrified we become of being exposed. That fear of being "found out" is a natural consequence of chasing flawless performance. When we build our sense of worth around getting everything right, the smallest mistake feels like a threat to our entire identity. That's where imposter syndrome digs in its heels.

This inner critic ignores your résumé and achievements. It waits for important moments and then whispers, *You've fooled them so far, but not for much longer.* It's both dramatic and annoying, like a coworker who won't stop reminding you that he or she is your "accountability buddy."

The fear of being "found out" is personal but also universal. Everyone, whether admitting it or not, has had that moment of crippling self-doubt. Maybe it's a big presentation, a family dinner in which everyone seems more put together than you, or the first day of a new job, The details change, but the script remains the same: *Someone is going to figure out I don't belong here.*

For me, these moments are especially vivid when I think about where I started. I didn't grow up with a storybook childhood full of piano lessons, trophy shelves, or ivy league aspirations. My childhood was more "duct tape and grit" than "polished and poised." Those roots made me resourceful, sure, but they also planted seeds of self-doubt. Growing up in Appalachia, where the world often treated us like the punchline of a bad joke, meant learning early on how to defend my worth (often to myself).

Fear writes its own script, but the person announcing my fraud? It's always been me. I'm learning to take the batteries out of that megaphone. I've worked too hard to let fear control my story.

But fear doesn't shout its insults and leave the area. It sets up camp. It follows you into every new opportunity, every big moment, whispering its one-hit wonder: *You don't belong here; they're going to figure you out.* So before we go any further, it helps to understand the cycle this fear locks us in. Psychologists have a name for it: *the imposter cycle.*

Introspection

What script has fear written in your life? Think back to a recent situation in which doubt showed up uninvited. How did it shape your actions or hold you back? Identifying these patterns is the first step in breaking free from them.

Breaking the Imposter Cycle

The fear of being found out isn't a visitor in your mind. It's an annoying roommate who never helps pay the rent, hogs the couch, and critiques your life choices every chance it gets. *Nice presentation, but everyone knows you got lucky. Why bother?* It's not only self-doubt but a full-blown campaign to convince you that exposure as a fraud is imminent.

This isn't general angst—it's the specific anxiety of being exposed. Imagine you're juggling flaming torches onstage when someone in the crowd shouts, "Wait! That's not a professional juggler. That's Karen from accounting!" You're dropping the torches, dodging the flames, and hoping no one notices that you borrowed the props from a kids' birthday party. Replace *juggler* with *parent, professional, boss,* or *friend,* and you get the idea. Fear thrives on these absurd scenarios, blowing every small imperfection into a full-blown circus act.

Psychologists call this "the imposter cycle," but it feels more like a hamster wheel where the stakes keep rising and the exhaustion never ends. The imposter cycle isn't a personal phenomenon. It's shaped by the environments we grow up in. Here's how it goes:

1. **The opportunity:** A new chance arises—that big promotion, a challenging project, or attending a potluck dinner for which you agreed to bring a dessert.
2. **Cue the fear:** What if they realize you don't belong there? What if your cheesecake cracks, revealing your utter incompetence?

3. **Over-preparation:** You rehearse, revise, and refine until your dog gives you a look that says, "You know they won't care about the frosting, right?"

4. **Execution:** Somehow you pull it off. The cheesecake is a hit or the meeting goes well. But do you celebrate? Of course not. You decide it was dumb luck, generous coworkers, or low dessert expectations that saved the day.

5. **Rinse and repeat:** Success raises the stakes for next time. Now they'll expect perfection. So the cycle starts again.

Sound exhausting? It is. Here's the cruel twist. Success doesn't break the cycle—it fuels it. The more you achieve the higher the imaginary stakes get. It's like climbing a mountain only to realize that the summit is a hologram, and the climb never ends.

For me, this hamster wheel has spun for years. I believed that relentless effort was the antidote to exposure. *If I work hard enough, no one will notice the cracks.* But fear isn't interested in how much you've accomplished. It doesn't care about your milestones or your triumphs. It's too busy shining a spotlight on every stumble, misstep, and typo.

This mindset felt natural while I was growing up in Appalachia, where the unspoken rule was to work harder, stay quiet, and avoid giving anyone a reason to doubt you. It wasn't about survival but rather about proving your worth in a world that was already inclined to dismiss you. The message was clear: You don't get the luxury of mediocrity.

Fear magnifies flaws and minimizes strengths. It's like that friend who says, "I'm just being honest," while listing every reason that you're doomed. Fear isn't honest. It's dramatic, turning a tiny crack in your confidence into a crumbling foundation.

Fear is also predictable. When it whispers, *They'll see you for what you are,* reply, "I'm a capable person who is still learning, like everyone else." When it hisses, *You don't belong,* say, "I do, and here's why."

Understanding fear isn't about forever banishing it. Let's be real—it's not going anywhere. But it doesn't have to call the shots. Fear might always ride shotgun, but you're the one behind the wheel. And when you see it for what it is—a sign that you're pushing boundaries and stepping into growth—it loses its grip.

Here's where things get tricky, though. Fear sits in your mind and demands action. Often it shows up as overcompensation, the relentless urge to work harder, do more, and chase perfection to mask your insecurities. It's exhausting and it doesn't work.

We'll dig into the costs of overcompensation later, but for now it's enough to recognize this: Fear often pushes you to overextend yourself, not because you're failing, but because you're afraid of being seen. I've felt this cycle play out in boardrooms and personal moments alike. But some of its deepest roots stretch back to when I grew up and what that environment taught me about worth.

Introspection
Reflect on a recent success. Did fear creep in and influence how you acted or felt about the outcome? How might breaking free from that cycle change the way you approach similar situations in the future?

Duct Tape, Banjos, and the Appalachian Tax
If Appalachia were a person, it would be the scrappy underdog in every feel-good sports movie, the kind that shows up to the big basketball game in mismatched socks and then gets laughed off the field. Then, when the audience thinks all is lost, it makes a three-pointer from half court. Appalachians have perfected the art of being underestimated and then turning the tables with a quiet *Oh, you didn't see that coming, did you*?

The thing is, growing up in Appalachia means you get two narratives drilled into you. One: You come from a place of unparalleled beauty and resilience. Two: The rest of the world sees you as somewhat of a laughingstock.

But this kind of duality isn't unique to Appalachia. Immigrants balancing old-world traditions with new-world expectations, or professionals navigating societal stereotypes about their fields know this push-pull all too well. It's a weird cocktail to drink as a kid. One sip makes you puff out your chest with pride. The next has you wondering if you should change your accent to avoid the inevitable *Deliverance* jokes.

For me, this duality came to life every time I ventured outside my small town. At home we celebrated our resourcefulness, our ability to hunt wild game, or heat our homes with the firewood we cut. But outside Appalachia? I learned that the world had a much less flattering script for us. We weren't resourceful—we were "hillbillies." Our traditions weren't endearing. They were "strange." And don't get me started on how every pop culture depiction of Appalachians involves either moonshine, banjos, or somebody's uncle who's also his or her cousin.

Those depictions? Except for the inbreeding (I have never seen or heard of any inbreeding despite living here my whole life), they're not wrong. They're incomplete. Yes, some of us play the banjo. I do, and it's an art form requiring years of dedication. And moonshine? It's as much a part of American history as it is Appalachian. Making it right takes chemistry, engineering, and ingenuity, not simple folksy charm.

Everyone's story risks being reduced to caricature when seen from the outside. Whether it's the misunderstood "starving artist" or the "numbers-obsessed engineer," stereotypes flatten complexity. They leave out the humanity, grit, and beauty that make identities whole. Every culture, profession, and community faces reductive labels that shape how people see themselves. And when those labels stick, they affect more than how others perceive us—they influence how we perceive ourselves.

This stereotype is as annoying as it is exhausting. It seeps into your psyche, making you feel you have to work twice as hard to prove you're not the punchline. When I first joined the Navy and boarded the USS *Camden*, a senior enlisted officer told a story about a guy from West Virginia on his last ship who supposedly never wore shoes until he enlisted—pure fiction, and not good fiction, the kind of predictable nonsense fools pass off as humor. When his story ended, he and the others in our circle looked to me for a response. I smiled and said, "Well, in my part of West Virginia we all wear shoes, but putting socks on for the first time at boot camp was special." It got the laugh I was aiming for, but it was self-preservation. Humor was my way of staying one step ahead of judgment. Self-deprecating humor was my armor. It was easier than risking someone else's judgment. But joking about my roots only gave others permission to do the same, reinforcing stereotypes I hated and feeding my own insecurities.

A while back I made a promise to myself: No more cheap laughs at Appalachia's expense. We've spent too long punching down on our own legacy, and it's time to rewrite the script. Books like *Storming Heaven,* by Denise Giardina, capture the truth of the people of Appalachia. Giardina tells of coal miners' fight for dignity, fairness, and survival during the mine wars of the early 1900s. The grit, the beauty, and the unflinching defiance in the face of exploitation are the story worth telling. It's not only an Appalachian story—it's an American story.

Appalachia's story is one of resilience born from necessity. It teaches adaptation, persistence, and the fight for worth in a world that often underestimates it. Resilience has a flip side. The fear of being written off, underestimated, or judged before you speak becomes the root system for imposter syndrome. You fear failure as well as the fear of proving someone right who already assumed you didn't belong. The fear of being dismissed does more than paralyze—it also fuels defiance.

That resilience became part of my DNA, but so did the fear of being looked down upon. Growing up, I internalized the idea that I had to be twice as prepared, twice as polished, and three times as humble to belong in spaces where others breezed in without a second thought. If Appalachia taught me anything, it's how to show up looking unassuming and leave with the trophy. But it also taught me to keep questioning whether I deserved to be in the room.

The echoes of this legacy show up in the strangest ways, as the time I gave a presentation and a colleague said, "You're so confident!" My immediate thought wasn't *Thank you*. It was *Ha! Fooled you!* That's the "Appalachian tax": Work harder, stay quieter, and make sure nobody realizes you're duct-taping it all together. When that's your baseline, imposter syndrome doesn't feel like a distortion—it feels like clarity. Your training has led you to believe that being yourself is insufficient, so you feel compelled to prove yourself in every situation all the time.

And yet for all the jokes and self-doubt, there's something beautifully defiant about our roots. We've carved homes into mountainsides while surviving corporate exploitation, natural disasters, and corrupt politics, not because we wanted to prove anything but because that's what survival demanded. This resilience became a defining feature of our culture. We had to do what was required and found pride in the struggle.

This defiance, rooted in survival and resilience, became part of my DNA. But over time I realized that the same defiance could become a double-edged sword, pushing us into overcompensation when fear takes the reins.

Again, this battle takes place well beyond the Appalachian Mountains. All people who are underestimated or misrepresented know how easily fear can push them to prove their worth or make them lose sight of it.

Over-Caffeinated Race to the Same End

If the fear of being found out is a hamster wheel, overcompensation is the energy drink that keeps you sprinting long after you should have hopped off. The logic goes like this: If I work harder, produce more, and stay two steps ahead, no one will ever notice I don't belong. But overcompensation doesn't quiet the fear—it feeds it, turning every win into another chance to be exposed.

Overcompensation often feels like the only way to keep fear at bay, but it can lead to burnout, or worse, behaviors you're not proud of. In *What Makes Sammy Run?* by Budd Schulberg, the titular Sammy Glick embodies this drive gone rogue, clawing his way to the top through ruthless ambition. While most of us don't bulldoze people to succeed, fear can still push us into patterns that chip away at our energy and integrity. For Sammy, the fear of being exposed drives every choice he makes. Deep down he knows he's an ordinary guy who got lucky. So instead of working harder or improving himself, he compensates by running faster, grabbing more, and leaving a trail of destruction in his wake.

Sammy's story is extreme, sure, but it's not alien. Overcompensation can nudge the best of us toward ethical compromise. Maybe it's taking credit for a team project because you're desperate for validation. Maybe it's staying silent when you see something corrupt because you don't want to rock the boat. Or maybe it's working yourself into the ground to meet impossible expectations, snapping at loved ones because you have nothing left to give.

I've caught glimpses of my own Sammy moments, as in the countless times I volunteered for projects I did not want to do, all because I thought I would look incompetent if I said no. In the end I became more tired, not more respected. Or the insane number of hours I have spent on PowerPoint presentations that no one ever reads— I'll lock myself into these detailed presentations with notes rivaling a Tolstoy novel's length. The reality? No one has the time nor the interest to go that deep on every slide. And then there are the things I'm not proud of: ignoring my family so I could train harder on my bike, hoping other cyclists would think I was fast. Meanwhile, no matter how fast you are, there's always someone faster. Or the compulsion to share everything I have ever learned, forgetting that politeness is better than being right. But shoot—I know things and I want you to know that I know them. In all of it I've tried to prove myself and at times I have lost sight of what I value.

Overcompensation is a losing game. It drains your energy and chips away at your integrity, convincing you that perfection is the only option and making you forget who you are.

The antidote to overcompensation isn't complacency—it's clarity. Ask yourself, *Am I doing this because it aligns with my values or because I fear what others might think?* Recognize that worth isn't measured by output or perfection. Learn to say no to fear and perfectionism, and yes, sometimes to the project no one else wants to touch.

Sammy Glick kept running because he believed standing still would mean losing everything. But standing still, taking a breath, and owning your imperfections lets you build something real. Sometimes standing still isn't about pausing—it's about planting your feet, reclaiming your space, and saying, "I'm not going anywhere." That's where defiance comes in—not the kind that lashes out but the kind that refuses to let fear have the last word.

Introspection

Consider how overcompensation has shown up in your life. Are there areas where fear pushes you to take on more than you should? What would shift if you allowed yourself the grace to step back and pause?

Putting Fear in Its Place

If the fear of being found out is a voice telling you to shrink, then defiance is the quiet, steady response: *No, I'm not disappearing.* Defiance isn't about yelling back at fear—it's about refusing to let it dictate your life. It's choosing to show up, flaws and all, and take up the space you've earned.

Defiance sets boundaries where fear pushes for overextension. Saying no to tasks that don't align with your goals or values becomes an act of self-respect, regardless of who ends up disappointed. Showing up as your true self defines worth, not productivity or perfection.

And defiance? It can take many forms. Often it's not a dramatic speech given to people in power. Sometimes it's allowing yourself that 2:00 p.m. nap, recognizing that rest will allow you to tackle the problems your tired mind is struggling to solve. We all need more of that type of self-care; a quiet rebellion against the voice insisting that if you are not grinding, you are not worthy.

Defiance could mean going after a career path or passion project no one seems to understand, like signing up for that pottery class because, hey, the world needs more lopsided coffee mugs. It might mean prioritizing a walk with your dog instead of the 8 a.m. conference call about late TPS reports.

These might feel like small acts, but they're monumental in a world where fear loves to shout more loudly than your instincts. Defiance doesn't have to come with fireworks. It must be real, though.

Every step of writing this book has felt like a battle with fear, complete with its own dramatic soundtrack. But I've learned that fear's greatest weakness is persistence. The more I show up, the more it must take a backseat. The decision to share my story, to talk about my struggles, to put my thoughts out there for anyone (friends, strangers, and yes, critics) to read? It terrified me. Fear told me that I wasn't ready, that I didn't have the right credentials, that someone else could do it better. But I kept writing anyway. Every word I put on the page was an act of defiance.

Writing this book has been more than a creative endeavor—it's been a declaration, an assertion that I'm done letting fear call the shots, that I'm willing to be honest, to be imperfect, and to own my story. Because if I've learned anything, it's that defiance doesn't have to be flawless, but it must be real.

Defiance is also about the power of a single word: *no.*

Defiance is about reclaiming your energy and focus when fear wants you to overextend.

It might mean saying no to tasks that don't align with your goals, setting limits that prioritize your well-being, or stepping back from perfectionism. "No" is a complete sentence and using it doesn't require justifications—it requires self-trust.

Defiance isn't just about boundaries. It's about challenging the ways fear keeps you small. Maybe it's speaking up in a meeting when your instincts tell you to stay quiet or pursuing a passion project no one seems to understand. Maybe it's taking a quiet walk, despite fear insisting that you have more work to do.

These acts might seem small, but they're really huge. Every time you choose courage over fear, whether through a boundary, a bold choice, or the quiet defiance of self-care, you take another step toward a life in which fear doesn't call the shots. If culture, class, or upbringing taught you that humility means hiding, then this defiance is radical. It's not arrogance. It's recovery. From years of being told to keep your head down, you get to lift it.

Saying no isn't selfish—it's intentional. Every time you use it, you're reclaiming your time, your energy, and your focus. You're telling yourself that your goals, your limits, and your well-being matter.

Every time you face fear and move forward anyway, you're practicing defiance. You're telling yourself, *I matter. My voice matters.* It's owning your worth.

When fear tries to convince you that you don't belong, defiance reminds you that you do. It's not about proving others wrong. It's about proving yourself right. It's about thriving despite fear. Here's the surprising part. That fear you're defying? It's not always your enemy. Sometimes it's the very thing that fuels your growth and pushes you toward what matters most.

Introspection

Where has fear held you back or kept you playing small? Jot down one situation in which setting a boundary or standing your ground could help you reclaim your energy or confidence. What's one small, courageous step you could take this week?

Wait—Fear Was Helping?

Here's something fear doesn't want you to realize. Its presence isn't proof of failure. It's a sign you are venturing into something that matters to you. The trick is recognizing when fear is steering you toward burnout, holding you back, or keeping you spinning your wheels. Fear clings to what matters most but can also force us onto the wrong road. It often drives burnout instead of progress. That's the actual price of fear when it's allowed to lead.

Unfortunately, fear doesn't come with an off switch, and most of us aren't taught how to keep it in check. Instead, it creates a feedback loop. You over-prepare to quiet it. You overextend yourself to outpace it. Then find yourself further drained when fear demands more.

This is where you need to stop and ask, *What is this costing me?* Because fear unchecked will take everything you're willing to give it.

Fear might feel personal, but it never stays contained. It seeps into workplaces, families, and communities, shaping how we treat one another and creating environments where anxiety thrives. When fear drives decision-making, it fosters cultures of overwork, perfectionism, and mistrust, making it harder for anyone to feel secure or valued. It often brings out the worst in individuals and entire societies: racism, sexism, classism, authoritarianism, and stigma in all its forms.

In fear-driven environments, relationships buckle under the weight of constant self-doubt. Teams fracture as people overcompensate, afraid to show vulnerability. Families struggle when fear turns expectations into impossible standards. And entire cultures stagnate when fear keeps us from taking risks, speaking up, or welcoming those who don't fit the mold.

Whether fear drives overwork, procrastination, or avoidance, defiance is your countermeasure. By stepping out of its shadow (in big and small intentional ways) you reclaim your story and inspire others to do the same. Every act of defiance, no matter how small, disrupts the cycles fear creates, replacing them with trust, courage, and resilience.

The actual cost of fear is systemic. It ripples outward, perpetuating cycles of insecurity and exhaustion that affect everyone it touches. If we want to break free from these cycles, we need to understand how fear shapes the spaces we inhabit and the lives we lead. Because addressing fear isn't only about reclaiming your story—it's also about creating environments in which everyone has the courage to own his or her fears.

Disrupting these cycles starts with individual action. By modeling vulnerability, whether it's admitting when you need help, owning your mistakes, or being honest about your fears, you create a space where others feel safe to do the same. Imagine a team meeting in which the pressure to appear perfect looms large. You might break the tension by saying, "I don't have all the answers yet, but here's what I'm thinking," or by sharing a lesson you learned from a past mistake. These small acts of honesty make you more approachable and signal to others that imperfection is part of the process, not a disqualifier.

Setting boundaries is key. For example, decline a project by saying, "Thanks, but I don't have the capacity for this right now." This kind of clarity models respect for your own limits while encouraging others to respect theirs.

These small acts of courage challenge fear, inspire others to rewrite their own scripts, and create a ripple effect of trust and resilience in your community. Because when you choose courage, even when your voice shakes, you're proving that fear doesn't get to have the last word.

Introspection

How has fear shown up in your life— through overcompensation, procrastination, or avoidance? Write one example and imagine how you would approach it differently if fear weren't steering the wheel.

CHAPTER 6

When Self-Doubt Turns into Self-Sabotage

Self-sabotage doesn't kick in the door wearing a cape and shouting, *Time to ruin your dreams!* It's way more charming than that. This voice shows up looking helpful and reasonable. *Maybe wait until you're more prepared*, it says. *Let's tweak this one more time before we share it.*

Sounds like a coach.
Acts like a friend.
It's not. It's fear with a clipboard.

Procrastination gets dressed up as patience. Perfectionism poses as "high standards." Overthinking struts around calling itself "being thorough." Self-sabotage often masquerades as good planning. You're not stalling—it insists you're being *smart*. What's really happening, though, is that you're getting stuck. Safe. Silent. Nowhere near where you want to be.

Imposter syndrome whispers, *You're not good enough.* Then sometimes it hands you a to-do list so long you never get started. One minute you're dreaming big; the next, you're knee-deep in hesitation disguised as preparation. That's when self-doubt grows into something sneakier: sabotage, the kind that doesn't need outside critics because you already have one living rent-free in your head.

I've battled this charming saboteur plenty of times, especially on the wrestling mat. After my dreams of gridiron glory slammed headfirst against the reality of my diminutive body type, I found an off-the-beaten-path sport that separated the small, gritty, wannabe athletes from the large, violent, traditional athletes. Somewhere in middles school as other boys packed on muscle and morphed into linebacker-sized powerhouses, I stayed about half their size. The football underdog story of an eighty-five-pound boy leading his team to state titles and being anything other than a suited-up water boy does not exist. So after the sport hit me with the classic *It's not you—it's me* breakup speech, I found my way to the wrestling mat.

This new athletic pursuit had weight classes, and no one expected me to strap a head-wobbling dome to my body. It offered a level playing field, pitting opponents of equal size against each other. This suited me fine. For the first time, I felt I had a fighting chance, and it became my new obsession.

Wrestling became more than a sport—it was a solution, a chance to prove to myself and everyone else that my size or my past failures did not define me. But stepping onto the mat didn't erase my doubts. If anything it amplified them. Wrestling became the perfect metaphor for how self-doubt and self-sabotage can intertwine.

Introspection

What does self-sabotage look like for you? Do you procrastinate, avoid challenges, or tell yourself you're not ready? Take a moment to identify the ways it shows up in your life.

Wrestling My Doubts (and Super Pickle)

Wrestling is a complex and full-body chess match. It's strength, strategy, and stamina all rolled into one sweaty six-minute battle. For me it was also a master class in how self-doubt can creep in and take you down before the match starts.

When I joined my high school wrestling team, I found a sport in which size didn't matter as much as grit and technique. Being small didn't mean I would be benched. On the mat it was me, my equally sized opponent, and the clock. Every win was mine alone to claim—as was every loss.

At first, wrestling felt like the antidote to all my insecurities. I trained hard, and by my junior year I was a significant force in the 103-pound weight class. My takedowns were precise, my endurance was strong, and I had a reputation for pinning opponents so swiftly that my team could count on six points whenever I stepped onto the mat. I had found my thing, a place where my size wasn't a liability and my grit paid off.

Then came Pickle.

Pickle, a wrestler from Petersburg (West Virginia) High School, was my kryptonite. He wasn't stronger or faster than me. He was simply impossible to beat. Every time we squared off it ended the same way: Pickle winning by a point or two and me trudging off the mat, frustrated and defeated.

I tried everything. I analyzed every move, studied his strengths, and practiced counters. None of it worked. Pickle's defense was impeccable, and no matter how hard I tried, I couldn't take him down. My bread-and-butter takedowns were useless against him. It became a mental block, a loop of self-doubt playing on repeat.

The rivalry became a running joke among my teammates, who took full advantage of my struggles. Teenage boys are experts at poking fun when you're down, and they did not hold back. Before the regional finals, I opened my locker to find a stuffed toy: a cartoonish "pickle" with a cape and a big red "S" on its back. Super Pickle.

A cousin of mine, who was also on the team, had left it there, and the rest of the guys thought it hilarious. I didn't. But as much as it irritated me, Super

Pickle was the perfect embodiment of my frustration. No matter how hard I tried, he always had the upper hand, always sprawled and countered every move I made.

By the time we reached the regional finals, I was physically and mentally exhausted. I felt the weight of every loss against Pickle, and I was running out of ways to break through. Then, before the championship match my dad, who had never wrestled a day in his life, offered me a single piece of advice: "Why don't you shoot as soon as the whistle blows?"

It was such a simple idea, but it differed from my usual approach. I was skeptical, but at that point I had nothing to lose. When the whistle blew, I lunged forward with everything I had and found myself deep into a leg hold. Within seconds I scored my first takedown against Pickle.

That one move shifted the momentum of the match. Pickle was as tough as ever, but for the first time all season, I beat him. It wasn't only a victory on the mat—it was also a victory over my own doubts.

That win felt like a superpower, not because I out-wrestled Pickle and won the regional championship, but because I out-wrestled the voice in my head that kept telling me I couldn't. It taught me that sometimes the best way to beat self-sabotage is to stop overthinking and just take the shot.

The guys loved it. Super Pickle became a mascot of sorts, a reminder of the ridiculous but rewarding battles that defined the season. While I had conquered Pickle, the actual battle, the one in my head, was far from over.

Wrestling taught me a lot about how self-doubt operates. It's not just the opponent in front of you whom you must beat—it's also the opponent in your head, the one making you hesitate, over-analyzing every move and fearing failure. After my big win, those inner struggles didn't disappear but followed me to the state tournament, where the stakes were higher and the pressure was greater.

Introspection

When was the last time you overcame self-doubt and acted despite fear? How did that feel in the moment, and what lessons from that victory can you carry forward today?

Why We Trip Right before the Finish Line

You would think beating Pickle would have launched me into a whole new mindset: confident, unstoppable, maybe a little cocky. That's not how imposter syndrome works.

Winning the regional championship should have been a catalyst. I had beaten Pickle. My teammates were cheering, and for the first time I had a title that felt significant: regional champion. I had worked hard for that moment, and I thought the win would silence the doubts that had followed me all season. Yet self-doubt comes with a catch-22. It doesn't disappear once you succeed. If anything, success turns up the volume.

The state tournament presented a whole different beast. Stepping into the Big Sandy Arena in Huntington, West Virginia, a massive venue, felt like entering another world. Buzzing with energy, the place had eight mats spread across the floor, each hosting simultaneous matches under bright, almost blinding lights. Spectators (parents, coaches, teammates, and fans) packed the stands, shouting encouragement or groaning in frustration as matches unfolded.

Everywhere I looked I saw confident wrestlers. They jogged around the mats. Their warm-ups were casual and precise. This was another day at the office for them. Meanwhile, I sat on the sidelines, trying to keep my breathing steady and my nerves in check. I had earned my place here, but it didn't feel that way.

My bracket held a returning state champion. I didn't need to face him to feel his presence looming over me. I caught sight of him jogging past. His fluid and effortless movements were enough to send my confidence spiraling. He didn't look like a 103-pound wrestler. He looked like a

Greek god in miniature, untouchable and unstoppable.

Imposter syndrome doesn't need actual evidence to take hold. It's happy to run wild with the smallest nudge. For me, seeing that state champion was enough to trigger the same mental loop I had been fighting my whole life. *What if I don't belong here? What if I blow it? What if everyone realizes I'm not as good as they thought?*

My first match went well enough. I beat an opponent everyone expected me to beat, and for a moment I thought maybe I had turned a corner. But by the time my second match rolled around, the doubts were back, louder than ever.

On paper the match should have been mine. My opponent wasn't a state champion and wasn't intimidating. But self-doubt doesn't care about rankings or stats. It whispers in your ear, distracts you, and saps your focus until you're simply going through the motions. That's what happened. My movements felt clunky and slow. I second-guessed every decision. So far in my own head it felt as if I were wrestling myself.

I lost.

In a double-elimination tournament, two losses mean you're done. My third match came down to overtime against another wrestler I should have beaten. By then, my confidence was so shaken that I forgot the one thing I was best at: takedowns. When the final whistle blew, I lost the overtime tie by default because I hadn't scored the first takedown. I recognized the irony. I had based my entire season on my strength in takedowns, and at the most important time, doubt stole that strength from me.

Walking off the mat that day was devastating. My junior season, which had started with so much promise, ended in defeat. Worse, it ended with my questioning every ounce of progress I had made. *Was I as good as I thought? Had I been lucky?* Or, worse, *had everyone else been wrong about me all along?*

Looking back, I can see the truth I couldn't see then: It wasn't my opponents who had beat me—it was me.

That's the brutal thing about self-sabotage. It doesn't wait for you to fail outright. It plants seeds of doubt so deep that despite your successes, you can't shake the fear that it's all going to fall apart. Sometimes that fear becomes a self-fulfilling prophecy.

I think many people can relate to this. Maybe you've felt that rush of doubt sneaking in as you were hitting your stride, as if the ground were unsteady beneath your feet. You aced a project at work, only to spend the next few hours picking apart your performance. Or maybe you found yourself in a relationship that felt right, but instead of enjoying it, you kept wondering, *What if I mess this up?*

Self-doubt doesn't discriminate. It shows up in big moments, small moments, and everything in between. As in wrestling, it's not always the external challenges that take us down but rather the opponent in our head, the one whispering that we're not good enough and we don't deserve to win. It threatens us by saying that it's only a matter of time before someone calls us out as a fraud.

The real challenge isn't beating what's in front of you—it's facing what's inside you.

For me that inner struggle didn't stop at the state tournament. It followed me into my senior season and beyond, shaping how I approached challenges in every area of my life. Wrestling also taught me something invaluable: *Self-doubt doesn't have to win.*

In the next section we'll explore how those seeds of doubt can grow into full-blown self-sabotage and why after a big win we sometimes trip before the finish line. Self-sabotage doesn't want you to lose—it wants you to stay stuck, and if you don't recognize it, that's what will happen.

Introspection

When have you let self-doubt hold you back when you were doing well? What would you do differently if you faced a similar situation today?

The Art of Quitting (Too Soon)

The state tournament crushed me. Wrestling had been my thing, the one place where success and confidence felt real. But the way the season ended confirmed all my worst fears. Losing matches was one thing; losing belief in myself was another. Self-doubt did what it does best—it fed me lies. Luck, not skill, had carried me this far. Maybe I wasn't good enough. Maybe I couldn't handle the pressure of success.

My off-season reflected this spiral. It wasn't as if I stopped training altogether, but I didn't approach it with the drive I had had before. I went through the motions without the same deliberate intensity. It felt like self-preservation. I now realize that I engaged in classic self-sabotage, protecting myself from future failures' sting by ensuring inadequate preparation. If I didn't put in my best effort, I wouldn't feel as disappointed, right?

Despite this, my senior year started strong. I had moved up to the 119-pound weight class and was dominating the regular season. I pinned my opponent in the regional finals and became a two-time regional champion. On paper I was having the best season of my life. But wrestling isn't only about strength or technique. As with the rest of life, it's about mindset. When the state tournament rolled around again, my old doubts returned with a vengeance.

The Big Sandy Arena felt as overwhelming the second time around. The crowds, the pressure, the constant buzz of activity, the multiple returning state champions—it was like stepping back into my worst memories from the year before. I could feel myself shrinking under the weight of it all. The mental spiral was so familiar that it felt like déjà vu.

By the third match, it was over. Doubts took control again, leading to another disappointing finish in my wrestling career. As if I needed more proof of how epic I had choked, the guy I pinned at regionals took third at state. This time the pain wasn't from the losses—it was from losing something I loved. Wrestling had provided a sense of purpose and a way to prove success to myself. That connection now felt severed.

Instead of regrouping and trying again, I walked away, telling myself that college wrestling wasn't the right path. With a good chance of making a team, quitting felt safer than risking another failure. Fear made the choice for me.

It took years to realize how that pattern of quitting too soon followed me into other areas of my life. In my twenties and thirties I saw it play out in my work, my creative pursuits, and my personal goals. Every time I hit a roadblock, that little voice would whisper, *Maybe it's time to cut your losses,* and too often I listened.

At work, this looked like jumping ship the moment a job became challenging or when I felt overlooked for a promotion. Instead of addressing the issue or sticking it out, I would convince myself that a fresh start was the answer. For hobbies, I would set my guitar aside whenever I hit a plateau in my playing. I wouldn't lean into the struggle or embrace the discomfort of pushing through a difficult phase. I would walk away and tell myself that I would come back to it later (though I rarely did).

Sure, I had grit in spurts. I could power through short-term challenges when the end was in sight. But when it came to the long-term focus, the three-to-five-year journey required to master something, I always seemed to cut it short. I would lose faith in the process before I could see the rewards.

Self-sabotage is sneaky, but it's not invincible. Wrestling taught me more than I realized. When your face is crammed into the polyethylene foam of a mat and you are about to experience an actual loss, you learn to push through discomfort, to strategize under pressure, and to keep going when you want to quit. That's the piece I missed for a long time: *You have to keep going.* Those lessons hadn't disappeared because I walked away from the sport. They were still there, waiting for me to put them into practice.

It took time along with a lot of trial and error, but I saw that self-sabotage wasn't about failing—it was about fear of trying, fear of succeeding, and fear of what might happen if I put myself out there. Once I understood that, I could start rewriting the script.

Instead of listening to that voice telling me to cut my losses, I started asking myself new questions: *What if the setback wasn't the end but part of the process? What if quitting wasn't saving me from failure but robbing me of success?* These shifts in perspective didn't happen overnight, but they changed the way I approached challenges.

I now see those moments of self-doubt differently. They're not proof I'm failing They're proof I'm stepping into something important. As on the wrestling mat, the key isn't to avoid discomfort—it's to face it head-on.

Inaction Is the Enemy, Not Self Doubt

Self-sabotage feeds on subtlety. Fear rarely introduces itself by knocking down a door. Instead, it sneaks through a window disguised as caution. Its tool is logic wrapped up with the voice of reason. The message sounds convincing: Playing small is smart; holding back is strategic. Staying stuck is not safety. That's surrender. The good news is that once you know what to look for, you can work with fear instead of letting it lead.

The first shift is recognizing when fear is behind the wheel—not the fear that keeps you out of danger but the kind that keeps you out of the game, the kind that shows up as you're gaining ground and whispers that you're not ready. It's the voice that tells you to keep editing before you hit "send" on an email, the one that nudges you to wait one more week before making the call, the one insisting that your idea needs more polishing before you share it. This fear does not protect you—it delays you. If you let it, it will derail you.

I used to believe the voice was wisdom, that waiting to feel ready was a mark of maturity. And then my dad gave me the single piece of advice before the biggest wrestling match of my life—to shoot first when the whistle blew. That advice broke the cycle. It reminded me that hesitation carries its own risk. I lunged forward and, for the first time took down the one opponent I had never beaten. The move wasn't elegant or well planned, and it was far from the most technically perfect takedown I had ever executed. It came out fast, raw, and instinctive. But it landed and changed everything.

That lesson stayed with me. Years later I scheduled a customer meeting for our sales team, the kind in which everyone from marketing to management had an opinion on the messaging. I kept tweaking the plan, second-guessing how to ensure that the conversation flowed, wondering if I was the right person to present. The pressure felt familiar, as in the seconds before a wrestling match. That moment came rushing back. I stopped editing, walked into the room, and led the meeting as I had rehearsed it the first time. No last-minute changes. No overthinking. The conversation flowed, questions landed, and the follow-up led to deeper engagement with the client. That wasn't a win on paper—it was a win over the hesitation that had almost held me back again.

Fear loses power when you act before it gathers steam. I noticed how often hesitation came from a story I had told myself. Before big sales meetings, I had run through worst-case scenarios: forgetting my notes, stumbling over my words, getting blindsided by a question I couldn't answer. I never imagined a different outcome. What if it went *well?* What if none of those fears ever materialized? If something went sideways, would it really matter as much as I feared? That shift didn't eliminate the nerves, but it gave me something else to focus on: what was in front of me, not the failure reel playing in my head.

This change in mindset carried over into my work. As I mentioned earlier, I spent much of my career tweaking presentations and adjusting phrases that didn't need adjusting. I told myself I was being thorough. My fear of being judged was the reason. At some point I woke up and recognized this pattern. After about the 9,000th detail on some minor report I spent way too many hours editing, I realized that no one had ever read everything I spent hours creating. I realized that I was chasing a finish line that kept moving.

Reading *Talent Is Overrated,* by Geoff Colvin, I learned that progress is the goal, not perfection. Colvin argues that greatness doesn't come from some magical talent gene. It is built on the back of deliberate practice. Athletes, musicians, business leaders, and other professionals at the top of their fields aren't perfect. They've spent years stacking small, imperfect steps until progress became undeniable.

That insight floored me because it was in direct conflict with what imposter syndrome preached. I used to believe the people I admired had been born with something I did not have, some recessive genetic fluke that made them better public speakers or free-throw phenoms. Colvin's book showed me the truth. These greats aren't gifted by nature. They moved toward expertise through messy forward motion. They allowed mistakes to happen and learned from them.

That's what builds competence and confidence.

Now when I finish a task I don't ask, "Was this perfect?" Instead, I ask, "Did I move the ball down the field?" That shift in focus changed everything. I stopped measuring success by polish and started measuring it by momentum.

Still, there were moments when the voice came back stronger. When that happened, I opened a folder on my computer filled with small wins. Emails. Notes. Screenshots. Things I had done well but would have forgotten without a place to store them. I didn't build the folder for motivation—I built it for memory. Because self-doubt is great at amnesia. It forgets your growth. It forgets your effort. That folder reminded me that I had done hard things before and could do them again.

Another shift happened when I changed the questions I was asking. I used to ask, *What if I fail?* That question invited fear into every room. Then I started asking, *What if I don't try?* That one landed harder. It exposed the cost of inaction. Failure felt like something I could learn from. Regret did not. That new question pushed me into conversations, into risks, into opportunities that scared me. It also helped me stay in the fight longer than I used to.

Self-sabotage is not a single moment. It is a slow drift away from what you want. The antidote is not inspiration—it is action. The smallest action you will take today is more powerful than the perfect step you plan to take next week. Doubt will always try to steal that moment. It will offer you every reason to wait. But you get to decide what to do when the whistle blows.

On the wrestling mat the whistle was my cue to act. It didn't matter if I felt ready or confident. When that whistle blew, it was time to move.

Life has its own version of the whistle, those moments when doubts creep in, when you face a decision and fear whispers, *You're not good enough.* The whistle isn't just a starting signal but is a reminder that hesitation isn't an option. Every time you act when doubt is screaming in your ear, you're building strength. That strength will carry you farther than you ever imagined.

Think of one place in your life in which you've been hesitating, not because you lack ability but because fear has been holding the mic. That's your whistle. When it blows, don't wait. Take the shot.

PART THREE

REFRAMING IMPOSTER SYNDROME

.

CHAPTER 7

The Secret Nobody Tells You

About fifteen years into my musical journey, I decided to do something wild. I started writing lyrics that turned into complete songs—not tinkering in a notebook but rather putting things down, sharing them, and trying to shape something honest. A friend of mine had written a few original tunes and encouraged me to give it a shot. So I did.

For a year or two we passed songs back and forth. He would send me a song. I would send back a song. Another buddy joined in, and it became a little circle of musical misfits, each of us trying to figure out what we had to say. It was creative, vulnerable, and fun. For the first time I felt that maybe this, writing lyrics, was my lane. It wasn't technical skill on guitar or banjo or fiddle that mattered (I don't have much). It was the words. That's how I've always made sense of the world. This felt like a place where I had something real to give.

About a year or two into this, I wanted to take it outside the safety of my own living room. I wanted to share these songs, these pieces of myself, with strangers. So I started going to open mics.

If you've never been to one, imagine standing in front of a microphone, guitar in hand, with your heart pounding as if it's trying to make a break for it. Every inch of your physical being catapults into a not-quite-panic attack, but your determination forces you to stay put and do the thing. It's more than a performance—it's a personal reveal. You're sharing more than music—you're sharing something that came from inside you . . . and everyone's watching.

The first few were rough. I would forget lyrics and hit the wrong chords, but I forced myself to show up, anxiety in tow, clinging to the idea that courage isn't the absence of fear but simply showing up with fear still riding shotgun. Over time I got a little better, a little more comfortable. But I never stopped feeling that I was about to be exposed as a fraud with a cape.

What I didn't expect was the community. Open mics, especially in small towns, are these incredible little ecosystems. The same people show up week after week, sharing the songs they've written, the covers they've practiced, the verses they're still trying to get right. We became a crew of imperfect artists, offering what we had. No pretense, just heart.

One night I saw a young twenty-five-year-old guy get up with nothing but an electric guitar. He looked a bit like Kurt Cobain's cousin and launched into a raw, gritty cover of early '90s grunge. Nirvana. Alone on stage. Just him, his voice, and a tangle of distortion and emotion. He *nailed* it. The angst, vocal inflections, and soul behind it all floored me.

After the set I walked up and said, "Hey, man—that was incredible. You brought a ton of emotion, especially in your vocals. It was powerful."

He lit up. Gratitude flooded his face as if someone had finally noticed him. "Thanks, man," he said. "I practice so much. . . . I never know if it's working."

That moment cracked something open in me.

Here was this confident guy on stage, crushing his set, and he was *still* second-guessing himself. He questioned his capabilities, a nagging self-doubt clinging to him, still fighting the same invisible war I had been waging.

That wasn't the only time I saw behind the curtain. The more I talked to other musicians, the more I realized *we're all feeling it*. Every one of them, from casual hobbyists to classically trained professionals, admitted to some version of the same thing: doubt, fear, and an internal voice saying, *You're not really a musician—you're pretending,* beating them down every time they tried to rise.

My vocal coach, someone with a degree in voice and a range that could break glass, once confessed that she still sometimes wonders what people will think when she sings.

That floored me.

This wasn't a fluke. It was a pattern. A quiet truth running under every performance, every brave creative act, every public risk. We all wrestle with it—the feeling that we're not enough.

Once you see it, you can't unsee it. All of them are walking around carrying their own versions of this doubt, trying to hide the fact that they're making it up as they go. That guy on stage? The woman leading the meeting? A coach, teacher, parent, manager, artist, neighbor? They're wondering if they're good enough too.

Famous, Brilliant, Still Unsure

It's not just the folks at open mics or the parents sitting in PTA meetings. That quiet voice of self-doubt? It doesn't care how famous you are, how many medals hang on your wall, or how many museum walls display your work. It shows up for everybody.

As highlighted before, some of the most brilliant, accomplished, groundbreaking people in history have felt like frauds. They've questioned their place, their worth, and whether they belonged.

You're in very good company.

Vincent van Gogh: The Tortured Visionary

Vincent van Gogh's swirling brushstrokes and vivid colors have made his work recognizable, yet during his lifetime his name was far from celebrated. Despite completing over 2,000 works of art, including masterpieces like *The Starry Night* and *Sunflowers,* he sold only one painting while alive.

Van Gogh's letters to his brother Theo reveal the relentless self-doubt that haunted him. He described "horrible fits of anxiety" and a consuming fear that his work would never matter. As he poured his soul onto canvas, the voice in his head whispered, *You're not good enough. You never will be.* That voice didn't stop him. Painting became van Gogh's act of resistance, his way of defying his inner critic. Each canvas he completed, each stroke he added was a quiet triumph over his own insecurities. His persistence transformed raw emotion into art that would resonate with generations.

Today van Gogh's legacy does not come from his self-doubt but from his refusal to give up. His story reminds us that what we create today may find meaning far beyond our own understanding. Self-doubt doesn't erase value. Sometimes it's the very thing that drives us to create.

Simone Biles: The Weight of Greatness

Simone Biles, with her gravity-defying routines and unparalleled athleticism, has become a symbol of human capability. With seven Olympic medals and twenty-five world championship titles, she has redefined the boundaries of gymnastics. Yet at the 2021 Tokyo Olympics it wasn't her dominance that made headlines. It was her decision to step back.

Biles experienced the "twisties," a dangerous mental block that left her disoriented mid-air. For an athlete whose success relied on precision, pushing through could have resulted in severe injury. However, she found stepping away difficult because her identity had long been associated with perfection and success. By prioritizing her mental health, Biles showed a different strength: the courage to pause. Her decision sparked a global conversation about the pressures placed on high achievers, particularly those in the spotlight. After years of dominance, Biles admitted that she still struggled with self-doubt. But rather than letting it define her, she used it to reframe what greatness looks like.

Her story reminds us that self-doubt isn't proof of inadequacy—its' evidence that we care about what we do. Greatness is about knowing when to pause, reflect, and protect yourself.

David Bowie: The Power of Reinvention

David Bowie wasn't born the cultural icon we remember today. Early in his career, he faced rejection, failure, and doubt. His first album flopped. Skepticism greeted his creative experiments, and success eluded him for years.

Bowie could have walked away. Instead, he chose reinvention. He leaned into his doubts, using them as fuel for creativity. Ziggy Stardust, the glittery, androgynous persona that catapulted him to fame, was more than an artistic risk. For Bowie it was personal. Ziggy became a way for him to explore feelings of otherness and uncertainty. Reinvention became Bowie's superpower. At the height of his fame he continued taking risks, experimenting with genres like soul, electronic, and industrial music. Though critics did not always acclaim every project, Bowie embraced the unknown, letting his self-doubt push him into uncharted territory.

His legacy reminds us that doubt isn't a stop sign but rather is an invitation to grow. By confronting his insecurities, Bowie turned reinvention into a way of life and left an indelible mark on culture.

Grace Hopper: Challenging the Norms

In the world of technology, where rapid innovation and high expectations collide, imposter syndrome is almost inevitable. Grace Hopper, one of the first women to make a significant mark in computer science, knew this all too well.

Hopper's work was pioneering. She developed the first compiler for programming languages and popularized the term *debugging*. But as one of the few women in her field, she often questioned whether she belonged. Her doubts didn't stop her. Hopper used her curiosity to challenge norms and push boundaries. "The most dangerous phrase in the language is 'We've always done it this way,'" she said. Her willingness to ask bold questions and defy tradition laid the groundwork for innovations that shape modern technology.

Hopper's story reminds us that imposter syndrome doesn't mean you don't belong. Sometimes it means you're challenging the status quo. Her doubts were part of her journey, and her courage to keep going defined her impact.

Why These Stories Matter

Whether it's van Gogh pushing through the noise in his head, Biles stepping back to protect her mental health, Bowie leaning into reinvention, or Hopper breaking rules that needed breaking, there's one common thread. They all felt doubt and didn't let it stop them. What matters isn't the doubt itself but how we respond to it.

Van Gogh painted through his despair while Biles protected herself. Both remind us that doubt doesn't erase value. It's the companion of every risk worth taking. Bowie and Hopper show that leaning into uncertainty can spark creativity and innovation. Together, these stories prove that self-doubt is universal. How we respond to it shapes the outcome.

You don't have to be an artist, athlete, or inventor to see this pattern at work. Imposter syndrome doesn't pick favorites. It finds its way into the everyday moments that define our lives. These stories remind us that self-doubt isn't exclusive to the extraordinary. It's a shared human experience. Whether you're spearheading a community project, navigating parenthood, or tackling a new challenge, the same principles hold true. Persistence, self-awareness, and connection can turn doubt into a powerful catalyst for growth.

Introspection

What about you? What might you create, achieve, or discover
if you stopped waiting for perfection and started showing up—
messy, imperfect, and human?

Everyday-Life Scenarios

Imposter syndrome isn't reserved for iconic figures or world-class achievements. It sneaks into the corners of everyday life, making itself at home in situations that feel monumental to us. Whether it's the first day at a new job or speaking up in a meeting, the doubts sound familiar: *I don't belong. I'm not good enough. They'll figure me out.*

Parenting: The Ultimate Freestyle Event

You've read the books, attended the classes, and pinned a thousand parenting hacks on Pinterest. Yet your toddler refuses to eat anything but Goldfish crackers. Your teenager rolls his or her eyes so hard that you're considering calling an optometrist. And somehow spaghetti sauce found its way onto your sleeve before a parent-teacher conference. At that conference you notice other parents nodding and swapping tips about enrichment programs while you're trying to remember which class your kid's in. You can't help but think, *They've got it all figured out. Why don't I?*

Parenting is less about getting it right and more about showing up. That you care enough to worry means you're already doing something right. Perfect parents don't exist, but good ones keep trying (despite the spaghetti sauce not coming out in the wash).

When my son was in fourth grade, I was finishing up the requirements for my master of business administration. Group projects, classes, and studying, all balanced along a full-time job, meant I wasn't home all that often. My march toward whatever absurd ambition I had at the time blinded me to the need to be present as a father and husband. On one of the rare occasions when I carved out father-son time, I threw a baseball a little too hard. Cainan, my son, didn't open his glove widely enough. The ball glanced off the side and he used his right eye to attempt the catch.

There was crying.

There were ophthalmologists.

There was a mountain of fatherly guilt.

Two decades later that moment (along with plenty of other entries in my "parenting mistakes" folder) looks different. Yes, I threw too hard. Yes, it did result in real pain for my child. Thankfully nothing permanent. But I was doing the best I could with the energy I had. I wasn't a perfect father, but I was *there*. I could have been there more often. At that stage of life I showed up as the best I knew how.

If I could go back, I would throw the ball more softly. Not too softly, but with enough restraint to avoid medical professionals when the inevitable eye catch happened. And I would do a lot of other things a lot differently. The biggest? I would be there a lot more often.

However, time machines do not exist. So I'm going to give that younger version of me some grace while the adult version of Cainan and the current version of me enjoy a laugh about all the mishaps. I'm still working on being a better father all these years later.

An Activist's Doubts

Tanya felt the weight of disappointment as she looked around the empty park. Despite her efforts to promote the community cleanup, only a handful of people had shown up. The voice in her head wouldn't stop: *This was a failure. Why did I even try?*

As the event progressed, Tanya noticed small but meaningful moments. A group of children learned about recycling, giggling as they sorted cans from bottles. Two neighbors who had never spoken before started chatting over a shared effort to clear debris. And a jogger passing by paused, asked about the event, and promised to bring her family next time.

That evening as Tanya reflected on the day, she realized something important: Success didn't have to mean a massive turnout. The connections formed, however small, had planted seeds for future change. She told herself that this wasn't a failure—it was a beginning.

From that point forward Tanya started reframing her efforts. She focused less on numbers and more on impact. Small wins, like one family deciding to recycle or a new volunteer joining the team, became reminders that change often starts small. Small actions, she learned, ripple outward in ways we can't always see.

Speaking Up in a Meeting

You're sitting in a conference room or on a Zoom call surrounded by colleagues who all seem to have something brilliant to say. You have an idea, but your brain insists, *What if it's stupid?* So you stay silent. Then someone else suggests the same idea, and everyone loves it. You're left kicking yourself for not speaking up.

Or worse, everyone else is tossing out ideas that stink. Meanwhile your idea is great. No one knows it, though, because you never shared it.

Be bold. Share your ideas. Not every idea—no one likes that person, who narrates his or her stream of consciousness in real time, turning a three-second thought into a hostage situation. You are not that person. So stop worrying you'll be mistaken for that person. Speak up. The room and the world need your voice.

Most people in that meeting weren't judging you anyway. They were too busy worrying about their own contributions. Sharing an idea isn't about being perfect—it's about being part of the conversation.

The Overachieving Student

Whether you're in high school, college, or grad school, the pressure to excel can feel overwhelming. You ace an exam but convince yourself it was a fluke. You stay up all night studying for the next one, terrified that your "real" abilities will show and they won't be enough.

One grade or one semester doesn't define your worth. Learning isn't about perfection. It's about growth. Every late-night study session and every mistake along the way is proof that you're trying, and trying matters most.

Imposter Syndrome in Creative Hobbies

You share a painting, a song, or a piece of writing with friends, only to second-guess yourself the moment you hit "post." When a friend praises your work, instead of your saying, "Thank you," you deflect: "Oh, it's not that good. I threw it together."

Here's a thought: What if you said, "Thank you"? Your creativity deserves to be celebrated—flaws and all. Real creativity isn't about perfection—it's about connection.

This one hits close to home for me. Whenever we create something new, we're taking a piece of who we are and releasing it into the world. That kind of nakedness feels terrifying when all we picture is the critics. But for every one critic there are a hundred people ready to cheer you on.

I've decided I want to live for those hundred. Forget the one. Life's too short to let a heckler have the mic. I would rather share who I am through conversations, through music, through creative projects like this book and trust that what I offer might connect with someone else.

A Writer's Revelation

Lisa hesitated before taking the stage, clutching her notebook. As she walked to the mic, doubts swirled: *What if it's not good enough? What if no one cares?*

Her voice trembled as she read, and the silence in the room felt crushing. When she stepped offstage, Lisa was certain she had failed. But as she packed up, a woman approached her. "Your poem," she said, her eyes glistening, "—it captured exactly how I felt after my divorce. Thank you for sharing it."

In that moment Lisa's perspective shifted. Her poem wasn't perfect, but it had mattered to someone. She realized creativity wasn't about flawlessness but connection.

From then on Lisa wrote with a new focus: *What do I want someone to feel when he or she reads this?* Her doubts didn't disappear, but she carried that woman's words as a reminder. Your work doesn't have to be perfect to make a difference.

Bridging the Gap

From activists doubting their impact to designers hesitating to share ideas, imposter syndrome thrives in the spaces between how we see ourselves and how we think others see us. The people around you are likely wrestling with their own doubts.

The mother who seems to have it all together? She's cried over burnt lasagna and missed soccer practice too. The coworker who exudes confidence? He's spent sleepless nights worrying about deadlines. Imposter syndrome lies to us, convincing us that we're alone in our insecurities.

Introspection

What's one moment where you felt like a fraud but kept going anyway? That, right there is proof of your resilience.

Self-Empathy: Treating Yourself like a Friend

We're all experts at empathy for other people. We reassure a friend spiraling after a bad presentation, remind a colleague that a typo won't ruin his or her career, and encourage a loved one to try again after a setback.

When it's us on the receiving end of failure? That kindness vanishes. We hold ourselves to a harsher standard. We're armed with a magnifying glass for every flaw and a running highlight reel of every mistake we've ever made. Why is it so much easier to offer empathy to others than to ourselves?

Harper Lee's *To Kill a Mockingbird* offers a timeless lesson in empathy. Atticus Finch, the steady moral compass of the story, teaches his children, "You never really understand a person until you consider things from his point of view . . . until you climb into his skin and walk around in it." This advice isn't just about understanding others. It's a call to see the world from a perspective different from our own, to look beyond judgment and toward connection.

But what if we turned that wisdom inward? What if we learned to "climb into our own skin" with the same empathy and understanding we offer to others? Too often we view ourselves through a distorted lens, magnifying our flaws and dismissing our strengths. Practicing self-empathy is about challenging that distorted narrative and treating ourselves with fairness, understanding, and grace.

It's something Harper Lee herself struggled with. After the success of *To Kill a Mockingbird*, she battled paralyzing self-doubt about her ability to write another book. Lee described writing as "a bloodletting," and although she started several manuscripts, she believed they wouldn't compare to her first novel. Who could blame her? She had launched her career with a masterpiece. The pressure of any follow-up effort left her in the strange position of feeling like an imposter compared to herself.

Her own battle with self-doubt makes her message of empathy more poignant. She understood the power of judgment, both external and internal, and used her work to explore the importance of kindness, compassion, and seeing things from another's point of view.

Practicing self-empathy isn't about letting yourself off the hook or avoiding accountability. It's about offering yourself the fairness and support you would give to a friend. Let's explore two powerful ways to start.

Rewriting Your Inner Dialogue

When my wife, Julie, decided to take up pottery, it was about more than clay. It was about courage. She had wanted to try it for years but kept bumping into the same doubts: *I won't be any good. All the others will know what they're doing. I'll look ridiculous.*

Still, she signed up for a local class. As she walked in, her nerves highjacked all her astute critical reasoning skills. The instructors were seasoned artists. Some students were regulars who knew their way around a wheel. Meanwhile, she was hoping not to launch a lump of clay across the room. Her inner voice kept whispering, *You don't belong here. What are you doing?*

Sure, she didn't produce a perfect pot on her first try. But the small, lopsided, not-all-that-functional thing she did produce was *a pot.* She laughed with classmates, got her hands muddy, and discovered that the joy wasn't in making something flawless. It was in giving herself permission to try.

A couple of years into her pottery journey, our house is full of her work. Bowls, mugs, vases—all stamped with her creativity. I love every piece she created and every piece she will still create. Each one is more than clay. It is a physical example of her growth, her risk-taking, and her willingness to push past fear.

Moving from *I must be perfect* to *I get to learn* was everything. The critic in her head quieted down, replaced by something gentler: *You're allowed to be new at this. You're allowed to be bad at this. You're allowed to enjoy it.*

That's the power of rewriting your inner dialogue. It doesn't mean you'll suddenly spin out a museum-quality vase. It means you stop letting the fear of not being "good enough" choke out the joy of simply doing the thing.

This shift in inner dialogue reflects one of the central lessons of *To Kill a Mockingbird*: the importance of challenging the stories we tell ourselves. Scout Finch learned to see Boo Radley not as a ghostly villain but as a human being, misunderstood and vulnerable. Examining our inner dialogue often reveals that fear, not truth, fuels the harsh stories we tell ourselves.

The next time you catch yourself spiraling into self-doubt, pause and ask:

- *Would I say this to a friend in my position?*
- *What's a more constructive way to frame this thought?*

Over time, this practice can shift the way you see yourself. Instead of a harsh critic, your inner voice can become a steady ally, one encouraging you to grow and perhaps enjoy a lopsided pot along the way.

Seeing the Bigger Picture

When we're in the thick of self-doubt, it's easy to fixate on a single mistake or challenge and let it define us. Harper Lee's personal story, as well as the story within the pages of *To Kill a Mockingbird*, reminds us to take a step back and see the bigger picture. Scout's understanding of Boo Radley evolves as she pieces together the full story of his life (his struggles, his kindness, and his courage). Her fear turns into empathy when she sees him in context.

We can do the same with our own lives. Think about a time when you overcame something difficult. It may have felt insurmountable, but looking back, you can see how it shaped your growth. The challenges we face aren't the end of the story. They're a chapter in a much larger narrative.

Imagine your future self five years from now, looking back on your current struggle. What would they say about your growth, resilience, or the lessons you learned? How might this challenge fit into the bigger picture of your life?

Julie applied this perspective in her pottery pursuit. Walking into a studio full of strangers and creating something from a block of clay felt intimidating the first year she started. In hindsight, though, it became a valuable turning point. She allowed herself to be seen as something far less than perfect. Instead of dwelling on her clumsiness, she embraced the learning process. With guidance from her instructors and deliberate practice, her skills grew. Over time, pottery shifted from a source of anxiety into a source of joy, something that grounds her, reflects her creativity, and has become a great part of her life.

When *you* feel consumed by doubt, ask yourself:

- *How might this experience help me grow?*
- *What lessons could I learn from this?*

Seeing the bigger picture doesn't erase self-doubt but it puts it into perspective. It reminds us that our worth isn't defined by one moment or mistake—it's built brick by brick.

The Power of Self-Compassion

Self-empathy is a practice, not a switch you flip. It requires intention and effort, especially in moments when self-doubt feels overwhelming. But the rewards are profound. Rewriting your inner dialogue helps you respond to self-doubt with kindness instead of criticism. Seeing the bigger picture reminds you that challenges are temporary and often pave the way for growth.

Extending grace not only to others but also to ourselves allows us to see our struggles through the lens of empathy. Then we can navigate imposter syndrome with greater clarity and resilience.

The next time self-doubt whispers, *You're not enough,* pause and ask yourself:

- *What's the kindest, most constructive way I can respond to this thought?*
- *How can I see this moment as part of my growth, not proof of failure?*

Empathy, whether directed outward or inward, is a practice of showing up when it's hard. By treating ourselves with the same compassion we offer others, we can reframe our doubts, embrace our imperfections, and take the next step forward.

Learning to Walk in My Own Skin

A few years ago I made the leap from a successful sales career into marketing, a field I was eager to explore but was outside of my experience. At first I convinced myself that my skills in managing relationships and delivering results would carry me through. Sales had been my comfort zone, where success was clear, measurable, and often immediate. I soon discovered that marketing felt like a different game with more cross-functional collaboration, a faster pace of activity, and a closet full of unknowns.

Each meeting seemed to highlight what I didn't know. Terms I had never heard flew around the room, colleagues rattled off strategies I couldn't yet grasp, and projects seemed to unfold at lightning speed. Doubt crept in. What if I don't belong here? What if this was a mistake?

I tried to quiet these thoughts with sheer determination, pouring myself into late nights and extra reading, but that nagging voice in my head wouldn't let up. It whispered: *You're not cut out for this.*

Then the tipping point came. My boss had to step away because of a medical emergency, and within weeks, two seasoned colleagues left the company. That left our team with three rookies, me included, scrambling to keep up. Overnight my responsibilities doubled, and so did the pressure to prove myself. It felt as if every decision, every deliverable carried the weight of the world.

One major responsibility landed on my plate: organizing a pivotal training event for nationally recognized, highly specialized physicians. This wasn't a casual meeting within the confines of some random office lunchroom. It was a cornerstone program requiring precision, coordination, and a deep understanding of complex science. These clinicians had agreed to help educate the larger healthcare community about the specific therapy we provided for a rare, life-threatening condition. With all our unplanned organizational changes, the task of training them as a group so they could train their peers fell to me. I told myself it was a chance to prove my worth, but a persistent voice in my head countered: *What if you fail?*

As the event approached, my anxiety climbed. Late nights blurred into early mornings as I obsessed over every detail. I convinced myself that preparation would be the antidote to doubt, but in truth, the pressure wasn't limited to logistical planning. It was personal.

My boss had designed the program and had planned to deliver the most technical aspects of the training. He had done it countless times before. Because of his medical condition, I needed to step in and present the most complex material at the event, a role meant for seasoned professionals. The audience of physicians were from elite institutions with decades of expertise. How could I measure up?

When the first day of training began, I was nervous. But I started off strong and got a few laughs, which helped ease my nerves. Then came the precise, intricate, and laser-focused questions. My confidence unraveled as I fumbled through my answers. Attempts at deflection only led to uncontrollable tangents. By the end of the day I felt exposed and unqualified. And honestly, I was unqualified to train this group of experts.

That night I found myself wide awake at 4 a.m., unable to silence the mental replay of every misstep. I wandered to the hotel gym, hoping movement might quiet the storm in my mind. On the treadmill, doubts haunted me: *How did you ever get into this situation? What made you believe you could do this? You belong back in a sales role.* The mirrors reflected my physical exhaustion along with the weight of my fears. At that moment I wanted to run away, leave the industry, find a plot of land in the middle of nowhere, build a log cabin, and never be seen by anyone ever again.

But I showed up for the second day of training anyway. I went through the motions on autopilot, disconnected from myself and barely engaged with the material I was presenting. I did not have adequate or confident answers to the questions the physicians never ceased to ask. It was objectively the worst event in my entire history of being in the industry. I knew this while the event was happening, and that made the dialogue in my mind more paralyzing than ever before.

When I landed back at my home airport, I felt deflated. I didn't simply feel that I had failed—*I felt like a failure.* In desperation I called a former boss, someone whose wisdom and steady demeanor had always grounded me.

Choking back tears, I poured out my frustration and self-recrimination, expecting him to confirm my worst fears. Instead, he listened and let the silence settle before saying words that felt like a lifeline:

"This doesn't define who you are."

He reminded me that the circumstances were extraordinary and that I had faced them without proper support. He explained that the so-called "failure" wasn't a reflection of my abilities but of the impossible situation I had to navigate. Then he told me what I couldn't tell myself:

"You walked into a storm and did your best to steady the ship. Don't confuse the chaos with your capabilities."

In that moment I realized how harshly I had judged myself. If someone else had shared the same story, I would have responded with empathy and encouragement. *Why couldn't I extend the same kindness to myself?*

It took time for his words to sink in, but little by little I saw the truth in them. During the training debrief with a larger leadership team, we identified structural issues as a major factor in the event's challenges, and I realized something startling: No one blamed me.

The failure I had carried wasn't mine alone. I loosened my grip on the self-blame and took stock of what I had done right. I had stepped up in a chaotic moment, leaned into my strengths, and stayed committed to learning when self-doubt screamed otherwise.

This experience taught me three invaluable lessons. First, I learned to counter my inner critic by focusing on my efforts, not my perceived shortcomings. Second, I discovered the power of leaning into collaboration, relying on my team instead of shouldering the burden alone. And third, I understood the importance of self-compassion. Instead of hearing *You failed*, I started telling myself, *You showed up. You grew. Sure, mistakes were made, but you learned something for the next time.*

In the months that followed I started building habits that transformed my relationship with self-doubt. Preparation became about more than logistics. It became a chance for me to ground myself. Before major events I began incorporating mindfulness exercises (a few minutes of deep breathing or visualization) to calm my nerves and remind myself of my capabilities.

I also began celebrating small wins. Instead of dwelling on missteps, I focused on what had gone well, no matter how minor. Seeking feedback from trusted colleagues helped me see my strengths and growth areas more clearly, reframing my inner dialogue from *I'm not good enough* to *I'm still learning, and that's okay.*

These practices echoed the lessons I had drawn from van Gogh and Biles. Van Gogh's persistence reminded me that showing up mattered. Biles's courage taught me the strength of knowing when to pause. Over time I saw myself not as a collection of doubts and missteps but as a work in progress, someone who could grow, care, and achieve while self-doubt tagged along.

The following year we hosted another training for many of the same physicians along with a few new ones. This time I pulled through every lesson from that earlier disaster. Instead of leaning on a well-meaning-but-without-a-formal-medical-degree internal employee like me, we partnered with a physician from a leading academic institution to handle the most technical aspects. I focused on what I did best: shaping the content, preparing the presenters, coordinating the details, and introducing the presenters. We also elevated our company's leadership by giving them a larger presence on stage, which helped participants feel more connected to our organization and to the shared cause that brought us all together. The training was a success, exceeding both our and the attendees' expectations, and for the first time I felt a measure of vindication.

We Are All Works in Progress

As noted earlier, imposter syndrome has a way of setting up shop in your mind, convincing you that every mistake is proof that you don't belong. It magnifies flaws, erases accomplishments, and turns ordinary self-doubt into a marathon of self-criticism.

As this chapter has shown, those feelings of inadequacy aren't unique, and they aren't insurmountable. Van Gogh and Biles show that self-doubt signals growth, not failure. Persistence teaches us the value of embracing the process, while courage reminds us that stepping back can be as powerful as pressing forward.

Recognizing that self-doubt is part of growth is a powerful realization, and it's only the beginning. Moving forward requires action like practicing self-empathy, reframing our narratives, and learning to celebrate progress over perfection.

Harper Lee's *To Kill a Mockingbird* offers us a fitting metaphor. Atticus Finch advised Scout to climb into someone else's skin and walk around in it. What if we turned that advice inward? Too often we see ourselves through a lens of harsh judgment, magnifying stumbles and ignoring strengths. What if we flipped the script instead?

What if we treat ourselves with the same understanding we offer others? What if we saw mistakes not as failures but as stepping stones? Self-empathy isn't about excusing missteps or avoiding accountability. It's about recognizing that any one moment, good or bad, does not define our worth. It's about seeing ourselves as whole, capable, and always learning.

Each time I've faced moments of self-doubt, I've learned that it's not about banishing doubts but about moving forward despite them, that showing up matters more than silencing those doubts. That's the point: The real you isn't defined by uncertainty but by your willingness to grow through it.

Introspection

What's one moment in your life when you doubted your ability to succeed but showed up anyway? How might that experience reflect your strength and capacity for growth?

The Real You

Life doesn't come with a scoreboard for belonging. Nobody is handing out trophies for perfection or keeping a tally of your mistakes. Most people are too busy wrestling with their own doubts to dwell on yours.

Imposter syndrome loves to convince you that you're an outsider, that you're one misstep away from being "found out." Your doubts aren't evidence of failure. They're proof you care. Caring is where growth begins.

Your journey isn't about proving yourself. It's about learning and growing.

Growth isn't linear, and it's uncomfortable. It comes with trial and error, missteps, and course corrections. But with each step forward you learn, adapt, and strengthen the foundation of who you are. The real you is defined not by your doubts but by your resilience in facing them.

Self-doubt isn't a solo act. You're surrounded by others who feel the same way, whether or not they admit it. Far from isolating us, imposter syndrome connects us through its universality, highlighting how deeply we care about what we do. In the next chapter we'll explore how that same care, the same voice that whispers, *This matters,* is your greatest asset.

CHAPTER 8

Imposter Syndrome as a Superpower

Over the years I've dabbled with several instruments, but the one that captivated me for several years, as I noted earlier, was the banjo. Yes, that's the five-string banjo. It produces high-tenor sounds when its strings are picked right. For an instrument that's become the unofficial mascot of Appalachian simplicity, the banjo is anything but simple. Its history, in fact, reads like an imposter syndrome case study.

The banjo's journey is about more than music. It's a lesson in resilience. It began as a West African instrument, carried across oceans by enslaved Africans, and adapted over centuries. Instruments like the akonting and ngoni, made from gourds and hides, were its earliest ancestors. Through time the banjo evolved, blending African, European, and American influences into something uniquely its own.

But its story wasn't without challenges. In the 19th century minstrel performers co-opted it, distorting its heritage and tying it to damaging stereotypes of Black culture. Later it became a cornerstone of bluegrass and folk music, with its African origins all but erased. And yet despite being misunderstood and reshaped, the banjo endured. Through adaptation and evolution it reclaimed its voice, ultimately emerging as a powerful symbol of musical resilience. It is wonderful to see how modern masters of the instrument like Béla Fleck and Rhiannon Giddens are ensuring the banjo's origins are taught to new generations.

The banjo is the perfect metaphor for imposter syndrome. The instrument has suffered from underestimation, misrepresentation, and misunderstanding. Yet its versatility and power are undeniable. As with the banjo, you've faced moments when others misunderstood or underestimated you or when you doubted yourself. The banjo earned its place in concert halls and living rooms by embracing its complex identity. You can too.

The banjo's story isn't just a metaphor for me—it became part of my actual story. In my life the banjo is more than an instrument. It's a reminder that what others see on the surface isn't the full story. As with the banjo, those of us grappling with imposter syndrome might feel out of place, but we have more to offer than we realize.

Introspection

What parts of your story, as with the banjo's story, are waiting to be reclaimed and celebrated?

The Dreaded Plateau (and the Tiny Voice that Said, "Maybe Quit?")

When I first picked up the banjo, I fell in love with its sound and complexity. I advanced at first, surprising my teacher. For a while I felt unstoppable. Then I hit a plateau. No matter how much I practiced, progress stalled. The intricate licks of my heroes seemed unreachable, and playing with others only amplified my frustration. Mistakes felt like proof I didn't belong, as if the banjo itself were mocking me.

I concluded at my lowest point that music wasn't for me. I believed only the talented could access music. Every missed note amplified the voice in my head that whispered, *You're a fraud.* Some days I wanted to give up on the banjo and music itself.

In retrospect, the plateau wasn't a failure but a sign of advancement. It reminded me that growth isn't linear and that persistence isn't about grinding. Growth is about pausing, reassessing, and finding joy in the process. Too often we mistake a plateau for proof we don't belong—when it's actually a chance to learn and grow.

Frustrated, I tried something new. Dave Asti, the same mentor who introduced me to the banjo, also introduced me to another lifelong love: the fiddle. Dave can play every stringed instrument there is and has been a wonderful guide throughout my entire musical journey. Switching to the fiddle wasn't only about trying something new. It was about shifting my perspective. The struggles I had faced with the banjo didn't disappear, but I saw them differently, and that made all the difference.

I didn't find that fresh perspective alone. It grew out of the stories, lessons, and inspiration I absorbed from a rich community of musicians who shared their own journeys with me. Their struggles and triumphs reminded me that every plateau is part of the process, a universal experience of growth.

Introspection

When you hit a plateau, how do you interpret it—as proof you're stuck or as a signal to try something new?

What Fiddle Legends Taught Me about Belonging

The fiddle brought its own frustrations, bowing right, pressing strings with precision, and avoiding the dreaded "dying cat" sound. My wife is the kindest person in the world because she put up with all the terrible sounds I created while learning that little devil box. Despite the challenges, the traditions that the fiddle represented captivated me. West Virginia's old-time music community became my refuge. The recordings and traditions of legends like Ernie Carpenter, Melvin Wine, and Wilson Douglas preserved tunes carried across generations. As I absorbed their stories and history, my love for the music deepened even as my playing stalled.

Two of my favorites who were still alive when I first started learning were Elmer Rich and Lester McCumbers. Regional legends in every sense of the word. Elmer lived a few blocks away from me when I was in Morgantown, West Virginia. He was a piece of living U.S. history. In 1936 as a teenager, he performed for Eleanor Roosevelt in Arthurdale, West Virginia, during one of her New Deal initiative celebrations. That story alone would have been enough to cement him in my mind, but Elmer was more than his past. He had a way of playing that transported you back in time, letting you feel the 1930s in every note.

In 2013 ninety-three-year-old Elmer Rich asked me to drive him to the Vandalia Festival in Charleston, West Virginia, where he planned to compete in the West Virginia Senior Old-Time Fiddle Competition. Though we weren't especially close, the two-and-a-half-hour drive flew by as Elmer shared stories. As I began driving, I feared there would be awkward silences. Elmer had other plans. He was eager to share his story with me. I was eager to hear it. He revealed his wife's distaste for the fiddle, his decades away from playing, and his eventual return to it. His passion never faded, waiting for the right time.

When we arrived at the festival the real magic began. Every three steps someone stopped Elmer to shake his hand, swap stories, or reminisce about old tunes. He wasn't only a competitor—he was a rock star in this community. I helped him to the green room, where he settled in with friends like Bobby Taylor, a celebrated fiddler and historian who has spent his life preserving this music.

As the competition began, I realized we hadn't discussed what songs Elmer would play. In fact, he hadn't taken his fiddle out of its case. When I asked if he wanted to warm up, he finally took the instrument out of its case, drew his bow across the strings once, nodded, and resumed listening to the other competitors.

When they called his name, Elmer shuffled onto the stage. I braced myself, certain that nerves or age or something else would trip him up. But the moment he lifted his fiddle to his chin, the youthful boy who once performed for Eleanor Roosevelt emerged. His first tune, "Colored Aristocracy," was a Rich family classic, played with a depth and authenticity that only decades of history could bring. His second, "Two Cs and an F," was another Rich family tune passed down from generation to generation, full of energy and life.

The crowd erupted in applause. Bobby Taylor leaned over to me and said, "Oh, he is *on* today!" Watching Elmer play reminded me that mastery isn't about perfection or talent alone. It's about showing up again and again, no matter how many decades life keeps the fiddle in its case. His resilience was a living testament to the power of embracing your identity, whether it feels out of place or arrives late.

As Elmer stepped off the stage, people rushed forward clapping, shaking his hand, telling him how much it meant to see him back up there. He grinned like a teenager. I'd never seen a ninety-three-year-old man look more alive. Shoot—I've seen thirty-year-old men less alive than Elmer was as a man in his tenth decade of life.

Elmer won his division that day. More important than that, he won the hearts of everyone who saw him play. On the ride home he was buzzing with excitement, recounting every detail of the day. For me it was the greatest music day of my life, despite not having played a single note that day. Elmer's story taught me that when self-doubt or life's setbacks make us feel out of place, our passions have a way of waiting for us if we're willing to return to them. His journey reminded me that the magic isn't in how long you've been away or how perfect your craft is—it's coming back, no matter what.

Elmer also taught me there are a lot of ways to travel into our later years. Too many people find their way to an easy chair, turn the television set on, and wait to die. During Elmer's last days he was trapped in a hospital bed. Another Vandalia Gathering was only a couple of months away. Although he was dying, the ninety-five-year-old Elmer kept talking about getting out of the hospital so he could compete in another West Virginia State Fiddle Competition. Never give up, you know? Keep chasing whatever it is that makes you feel alive.

Introspection

What passion have you set aside that's waiting for
you to return to?

This experience taught me something profound. My love for old-time music had brought me into a community where I could connect with legends, share stories, and feel part of something bigger than myself. My playing wasn't extraordinary, but my passion and persistence had given me a seat at the table. That, I realized, was its own kind of success.

Although they weren't formal mentors, I made it a point to place myself around excellent musicians. Elmer Rich was one of the living legends who left an imprint on me, but there were others who became friends and sources of inspiration. Chris Haddox, for instance, is an incredible fiddler who also plays folk-style guitar and writes beautiful songs. Through Chris I saw the broader world of music, beyond the banjo and fiddle, and explored all the elements that go into creating something meaningful. The key word here is *creating*. Chris doesn't simply play music—he makes it, shapes it, and shares it, which inspires me to think differently about my relationship with music.

During this time I met Ben Townsend, who played fiddle in the band Fox Hunt, an up-tempo group that fused old-time traditional music with modern energy and ideas. Ben's fiddle was the glue that held it all together. Watching him play with such skill and passion was a revelation. About a decade later, Ben became perhaps the most important person in my entire music journey. That's a story for the final chapters of this book.

What I can say now is that being around people like Elmer, Chris, Dave, Ben, and many others kept me going when I wanted to give up. Their talent, passion, and generosity with their time reignited my love for music over and over again. While I often felt inferior to them, as if I didn't belong in the same room, much less in the same jam circle, their presence pushed me forward. They demonstrated that music's magic transcends a single instrument or style.

These mentors helped me understand the link between my love for musicians like John Prine and Bob Dylan and the musical traditions of other legends, including Wilson Douglas and Elmer Rich. At first these influences felt worlds apart, but I saw how they could blend into something personal, something mine. I still didn't know where I fit within the broader world of music, but for the first time I could feel that I belonged somewhere.

The connection wasn't just to the songs or the techniques. It was to the living tradition they represented. Yet as I embraced this sense of belonging, the familiar feelings of inadequacy lingered. It wasn't until I started writing my own songs that I found my place.

Elmer, Chris, and the other legends taught me that greatness isn't about flawless technique but rather about having the courage to embrace your own voice. For me, that courage came through songwriting, the discovery of which would redefine my relationship with music.

As much as I admired others' artistry, their stories slowly pointed me toward a question I hadn't dared to ask: What would happen if I stopped trying to play like *them* and started playing like *me*?

When I Finally Stopped Trying to Sound like Someone Else

For a long time I let comparison rob me of the joy that music was supposed to bring. Whether it was banjo, fiddle, or any other instrument I picked up, I couldn't shake the feeling that I wasn't good enough. I would listen to my heroes like Béla Fleck, Dave Asti, or Elmer Rich and convince myself that I was wasting my time. If I couldn't match their mastery, what was the point?

My confidence tanked in the most spectacular fashion. I wallowed in the basement of doubt, unable to play the simplest songs I had learned in my first few weeks. It got to the point in which I didn't want to play in front of myself, let alone others. I stopped opening the case for weeks. I avoided the jams I used to love. The silence grew louder than any wrong note I might have played. On the rare occasions when my confidence crept back to a relative peak, I would cling to the basics like a lifeline. I leaned on boring, safe riffs, too paranoid to step outside my comfort zone. My creativity often felt slow and clumsy, but as with an earthworm enriching the soil, those moments laid the groundwork for growth.

In my mind, performing meant perfection. If I hit one wrong note, I thought someone would notice. When they noticed, they would think I was terrible. The idea of performing as anything less than flawless made me feel like a fraud. It was paralyzing. Music had started as a source of fun, but this pressure drained every ounce of joy from it.

Despite the frustration, I couldn't let go of the hope that music still held something for me. Then something shifted when I discovered songwriting. For the first time, I stopped measuring my worth against someone else's skills. Instead of trying to mimic the greats, I found my way to connect with music. Through words and melodies, I could tell my own stories—stories that didn't require a dazzling technique or decades of experience, only a willingness to be honest and vulnerable.

Songwriting was a revelation, a door into the world of music I had long admired but never felt part of. As I wrote, my confidence grew, not from perfection but from authenticity.

Ironically, the more I focused on songwriting, the easier playing became. The banjo stopped feeling like a battlefield, the fiddle felt less intimidating, and the guitar came rushing back into my life. Free from the comparison trap, I could enjoy the music itself.

I came to realize that the problem was my mindset. I had spent years holding myself to impossible standards, thinking I had to play "Two Cs and an F" like Elmer or nail every lick like Dave. Those players hadn't been born with their skills. They had honed them over decades. Elmer didn't become Elmer overnight. He played the same songs for ninety years. I had been expecting myself to measure up to that level of mastery after a handful of years. It was absurd, but in the moment it felt like reality.

This shift in perspective was liberating. I appreciated my sound, imperfections and all. When I stopped trying to replicate someone else's greatness, I found my voice, whether it was on the banjo, the fiddle, or through a song I had written.

As my perspective shifted, so did my definition of success. No longer was perfection my goal. Success became about expression, about translating my emotions into music in a way that felt authentic. I noticed something remarkable: In the rare moments when I could let go of the pressure and feel the music, people reacted.

One of the first songs I ever wrote, "You and Me," captured the fleeting nature of life and love — a sentimental melody about meeting someone special and watching time slip away. It resonated more than I had expected. After performing it for a small audience of friends, I looked up to find everyone sitting in silence staring back at me. Lost in the music, I hadn't noticed much while I was performing it. I had a moment of panic thinking their non-response showed their distaste of the song. Then one of them spoke up and said, "That was beautiful. It's my favorite one so far." The song connected; it moved them, and the realization amazed me.

That moment gave me a glimpse of what I had always been searching for. For the first time I understood that my music didn't need to match someone else's to matter. It could connect with people because it was mine, because it came from a genuine place.

Imposter syndrome whispered, *I don't belong*, but it also pushed me to experiment and grow in ways I never would have otherwise. It became less about perfection and more about authenticity.

The process wasn't fast or easy. It took years to unlearn the belief that performing meant perfection. It took longer to see myself as a musician— not because I mastered an instrument but because I had something to say. I discovered the unique contributions I could make, not despite my imperfections but because of them.

Songwriting became my way forward. It was no longer about how many notes I could play or how clean my technique was. It was about connection, about creating something that felt real. The more I embraced that, the more I realized music didn't have to be perfect to matter. It had to be honest. This realization didn't come without struggle. Years of grappling with doubt revealed how imposter syndrome could be a catalyst for growth, driving me forward when I felt unready.

The Surprising Upside of Doubt: Progress

For years I thought imposter syndrome was the enemy. It whispered that I didn't belong and replayed every mistake in a loop. But over time I saw what doubt had really done: It had pushed me to practice harder, learn more, and grow in ways I never would have if I had started out confident. That tension between fear and drive may have slowed me down, but it also shaped me.

Growth didn't come from feeling ready. It came from showing up anyway. Doubt made me work smarter, dig deeper, and keep going long after I wanted to quit. Looking back, I realize that imposter syndrome was more than a hurdle—it was part of the fuel.

This wasn't some quick breakthrough or feel-good "aha" moment. It was twenty years of stop-and-go progress, plateaus, and questioning whether I should give it up. All of it was messy, frustrating, and real.

Imposter syndrome is relentless and overcoming it takes genuine effort. There's no overnight fix or single revelation that will erase it. The process is challenging. It requires time, persistence, and the courage to keep showing up when doubt tries to convince you otherwise.

I realize now how imposter syndrome was both my greatest challenge and my greatest motivator. It pushed me to practice harder, explore new instruments, and connect with my community. But it wasn't easy.

There were days when the gap between where I was and where I wanted to be felt overwhelming. Imposter syndrome thrived in that gap, pointing out how far I still had to go. But what I didn't realize at the time was that the gap wasn't a sign of failure—it was a sign of growth.

That growth was messy, frustrating, and full of false starts. It was also meaningful. Every hour of practice, every misstep, every moment of wanting to quit all added up to something greater than the sum of its parts.

Introspection

What if your self-doubt isn't a barrier—but a signal?

As with the banjo's journey, your moments of uncertainty could guide you toward reinvention, resilience, and something greater than what you imagined. Think about a time when doubt made you hesitate. What if you had leaned into that feeling and used it to try something new? That's the challenge that imposter syndrome presents. It asks you to keep going when you don't feel ready.

So if you're reading this and thinking, *When will this get easier?* the honest answer is—I don't know. It might take years. It might take decades. The fact that you're in the game, grappling with self-doubt and still showing up, means you're already growing.

Making Peace with Your Inner Critic

I spent most of my life thinking the battle with imposter syndrome was about silencing self-doubt and fighting the inner critic until it gave up. Trying to fight my mind was exhausting. Every thought of inadequacy felt like a tug-of-war I could never win.

That's when I stumbled across Eckhart Tolle's *The Power of Now*. I didn't pick it up expecting it to change my life. I grabbed it because a friend recommended it. The title sounded interesting, and I thought it might help with my constant overthinking. What I didn't realize was that Tolle's ideas would give me a new perspective on how to live with imposter syndrome.

Instead of treating my inner critic like an enemy to defeat, I started learning how to live with it. Tolle's teachings on mindfulness, presence, and acceptance weren't abstract concepts; they became practical tools I could use every time self-doubt threatened to take over. These small practices didn't fix everything overnight, but they helped me reframe how I approached music, creativity, and life itself.

Tolle's work taught me that presence goes beyond mindfulness. It's about rediscovering joy when doubt is loudest. As with the banjo's story of adaptation, his teachings revealed that resilience is rooted not in perfection but in embracing one's current state, flaws included. Here's how his insights helped me find peace during some of my most challenging moments:

Separating Thought from Truth

I first practiced observing my thoughts during a solo banjo session that was going wrong. I had botched the same tricky lick five times in a row, and my mind was spiraling: *Why bother? You'll never get it right.* I caught myself in the middle of the storm, paused, and thought, *Oh, there's that thought again.* That simple shift, labeling the criticism as a thought, not a truth, helped me shake off the frustration. Instead of giving up, I approached the piece with fresh focus and patience.

This practice reminded me that my inner critic doesn't have to run the show. Observing those negative thoughts and letting them pass are often enough to regain perspective.

> THE REFRAME: The next time self-doubt creeps in, pause and label it. Instead of believing the thought, say to yourself, *Oh, there's that thought again.* Treat it like background noise, acknowledge it, and then refocus on what you were doing.

Focusing on Breath

Before a nerve-wracking community jam session, I could feel panic settling in. My palms were sweaty, my heart raced, and the voice in my head whispered, *You're about to mess this up.* I remembered Tolle's advice to focus on the breath as an anchor. Closing my eyes, I took three slow, deep breaths. With each exhale I felt my shoulders relax, and my focus shifted from fear to music.

I grounded myself enough to play. I wasn't flawless, but I was present. That made all the difference.

> THE REFRAME: Before your next high-stakes situation (whether it's a presentation, performance, or tough conversation) take three slow, deep breaths. As you inhale, count to four. As you exhale, count to four. Let your breath anchor you in the moment.

Sensing the Inner Body

During one frustrating fiddle session, I couldn't get my bowing to cooperate. My fingers felt clumsy, and my notes sounded harsh. Instead of forcing it, I paused and shifted my focus to the sensations: the weight of the bow in my hand, the vibration of the strings under my fingers. I stopped worrying about how it sounded and tuned into how it felt.

That moment grounded me. The frustration was gone, swapped for the simple joy of playing. Not performing. Not perfecting. Just playing.

> **THE REFRAME:** The next time frustration builds, shift your focus to physical sensations. Feel your feet on the ground, your hands gripping an object, or the rhythm of your breath. Grounding yourself in your body can quiet the mental noise.

Accepting the Present Moment

Acceptance was one of the hardest lessons for me to learn. Music placed it under a large spotlight. I always wanted to push harder, get better, and hit the next milestone. During one bad practice session I couldn't get through a simple tune. My instinct was to grit my teeth and fight through, but I stopped and told myself, *This is where I am right now, and that's okay.*

It wasn't a magic fix. The frustration didn't disappear. But it softened enough for me to keep going without the usual self-criticism. Accepting where you are isn't about giving up—it's about making peace with the process and allowing yourself to grow.

> **THE REFRAME:** When you find yourself resisting where you are, say out loud (or in your head), *This is where I am right now, and that's okay.* Repeat it until the tension softens. Progress starts with acceptance.

Letting Go of Psychological Time

One of my first group performances taught me the importance of staying present. Before we started, I was stuck in a thought loop: *What if I mess up? What if everyone notices?* The hypothetical disaster consumed my every thought, paralyzing me. Then I asked myself, *What can I do right now?*

That shift, from worrying about the entire performance to focusing on the next chord, got me through the set. Staying in the moment wasn't only helpful—it was essential.

> **THE REFRAME:** The next time you spiral into *what-if* scenarios, stop and ask, *What can I do right now?* Redirect your energy to the next small action. Focusing on the present keeps anxiety from running the show.

Practicing Stillness and Silence

Some of my most profound moments with music didn't involve playing at all. Sitting with my banjo, appreciating its weight and texture, or listening to the natural hum of the strings brought me a sense of clarity I couldn't find through practice alone.

Stillness isn't about silence—it's about creating space. Those quiet moments became the foundation for deeper creativity and connection with my music.

> **THE REFRAME:** Spend five minutes doing absolutely nothing—no phone, no music, no distractions. Sit, breathe, and notice what happens. Stillness fuels creativity and clarity.

Embracing Nature

When doubt felt overwhelming, I took my banjo or fiddle outside and sat under a tree. The rustle of leaves, the smell of the earth, and the sound of birds singing grounded me in a way nothing else could. Practicing in nature made the music feel less like a task and more like communion with the moment.

It wasn't about getting the notes right. It was about being part of something bigger.

> **THE REFRAME:** Step outside for five minutes today. Feel the sun or wind on your skin, listen to the surrounding sounds, and breathe deeply. Nature will remind you that you don't need to rush or perfect everything.

Each of these tools gave me a way to navigate doubt not as something to eliminate but as something to understand.

And that changed everything.

These practices didn't make imposter syndrome disappear overnight. But they taught me to approach it differently, as part of the process, not a flaw to be fixed. Each small step toward mindfulness helped me reconnect with the joy of music and life.

Introspection

When was the last time you let yourself pause and breathe? What might happen if you gave yourself permission to take things one moment at a time?

Doubt Isn't Dead Weight—It's a Signal to Move

These practices don't eliminate imposter syndrome, but they've helped me see it for what it is: a part of me, not the whole of me. By grounding myself in the present moment, I've found freedom from the weight of the past and the anxiety of the future.

The banjo's story proves that the underestimated can rise to something extraordinary with the right chance. You hold the same potential—to reinvent, to grow, to thrive. Imposter syndrome isn't a flaw. It's friction that creates movement. It sharpens your focus and forces you to adapt, to invent, to stretch beyond what's comfortable. That uncomfortable tension between self-doubt and forward motion? That's where creative breakthroughs live. The very thing that makes you hesitate is the same thing that can make you better. Keep moving forward. As with the banjo, your voice deserves to be heard. Play your song, imperfections and all.

CHAPTER 9

Your Greatest Hits (and Misses)

If my life were an album, I would want it to be a flawless "greatest hits" collection, the kind in which every track is a banger, every moment a highlight. No awkward pauses, no questionable decisions, no songs titled "Oops—That Wasn't on Mute."

But life doesn't work like that.

Instead, it's more like one of those deluxe editions. Some chart-toppers, some deep cuts, and a few tracks so questionable that you wonder, *What was I thinking?*—songs that should have stayed in the vault, the ones you would rather skip.

Yet without them the album wouldn't be complete.

That's the problem with how we see ourselves. We zoom in on the off-key moments, the failures, the embarrassing memories, the things we wish we could erase. Meanwhile, the successes? The moments when we nailed it? We treat those like lucky accidents, things that don't "count." Imposter syndrome thrives on this selective memory, convincing us that our worst moments define us while our wins are flukes.

That's a lie.

Life isn't a highlight reel. It's a full album, messy and unpredictable.

Nobody knew that better than John Prine.

We all love a good success story, one that comes with a slow-motion training montage, a triumphant soundtrack, and a final scene in which the underdog gets the recognition he or she deserves. But real life doesn't wrap things up so neatly. John Prine understood this. In his song "That's the Way the World Goes 'Round," the chorus lays it out, saying, "That's the way the world goes 'round. You're up one day and the next you're down"—noting that you're in only half an inch of water yet you think you're going to drown.

Some days you're thriving, landing promotions, crushing deadlines, getting compliments that you believe. Other days you're tripping over yourself, emailing the wrong person, realizing too late that you've been walking around with toilet paper stuck to your shoe or feeling like a fraud when the evidence suggests otherwise.

Yet when we look back at our lives, we don't see the full picture. For those of us wrestling with self-doubt, the failures are the ones stuck on repeat, while the chart-toppers do not get airplay.

We've all had those moments of feeling stranded, stuck, exposed. Maybe you bombed a big sales meeting. Maybe you blurted out something ridiculous during an important lunch and wished for a time machine. Maybe you made a massive decision and realized, *Oh, no—I've made a huge mistake!*

That's the heart of imposter syndrome, isn't it? It's the fear that people are watching, judging, noticing every misstep, that deep, sinking worry that everyone else has figured out while you're the fool sitting there naked, waiting for someone to call you out.

But those so-called flops are not as bad as they seem.

The ice that has you frozen in place always breaks. Those moments never last as long as they feel. We survive our worst moments. We shake them off and move forward. Later, if we're lucky, we laugh at how serious it all seemed.

Still, if my brain were to edit the highlight reel of my life, it wouldn't be a showcase of achievements. No inspiring career milestones, no moments of resilience, no well-earned victories. Instead, it would be a montage of—

- That first sales call with a physician when I could barely utter my name;
- Every time I've forgotten the name of someone I knew from my past and tried to fake my way through the conversation;
- Last week when I backed the car into the corner of the garage.

Meanwhile, my actual accomplishments that required effort, skill, and perseverance barely register. My brain waves them off as luck, timing, or not that big of a deal. And sometimes it's worse than dismissal. Sometimes my brain loses them. They drift into some Bermuda Triangle of accomplishment disappearances, never to be seen again. I could run into someone years later who says, "Remember when you _____?" and I'll stare blankly, because my brain tossed that success overboard like excess baggage.

If someone else told me he or she had overcome a rough childhood, served in the Navy, worked his or her way through college in two and a half years, built a career in pharmaceuticals and biotech, and raised a family along the way, I would call the person incredible. But when it's me? My brain shrugs and says, *Yeah, but remember one time you mispronounced "quinoa" at a dinner party and kept going like you were right?*

This is the trap of imposter syndrome. It distorts reality. Our worst moments feel like the truth while our successes seem like luck. That's why we lie awake at night, replaying every awkward thing we've ever done but struggle to recall the times we rose to the occasion.

If we take a step back, the truth is obvious.

Nobody's album is all greatest hits. Everybody has B-sides—the songs that didn't quite land, the lyrics that could have been better, the half-finished moments that never made it to the radio. They're still part of the music.

Introspection

When you look back at your own "album," which moments do you replay the most? Are they your wins or your misses?

If John Prine was right, if life is a constant cycle of up and down, of winning and losing, of thinking you're drowning only to realize the water is only slightly up to your ankles . . . maybe it's time you stop treating your missteps like proof you have somehow failed.

Maybe instead they are proof you were in the game all along.

Some B-sides are a little embarrassing. Others feel like a complete disaster. And when I think about my life, one track stands out above the rest . . .

How to Burn Your Life Down and Learn Something in the Process

There are moments in life when you can hear the dramatic record scratch in the background, followed by a narrator saying, "Yep, that's me. You're probably wondering how I got here."

For me, that moment was sitting on a park bench in Florida, staring at my shattered bank account, wondering how I had blown up my career, uprooted my family, and walked straight into one of the most spectacular failures of my life.

Let's rewind.

On paper, this was supposed to be a success story. My wife and I had an exciting plan: Move to Florida, partner with my brother-in-law Jay in his booming trucking business, and achieve that magical thing people call financial security. I had recently finished an MBA, and this move felt like the next big step, the kind of calculated risk responsible and successful adults make.

At first it seemed perfect. Jay had connections. I had a business background, and my wife was thrilled to be closer to her parents. This wasn't a career move. This was the moment when everything was supposed to click into place.

It did not click.

Almost immediately cracks started forming. My thirteen-year-old son, ripped from the only home he had ever known, struggled to adjust to a new school. My wife, once excited about being near family, missed the life we had built in Morgantown, West Virginia.

Then there was the business itself. Jay and I realized our work styles couldn't have been more different. He thrived in a high-pressure, detail-obsessed environment where he maintained constant control. I, on the other hand, worked best with autonomy, trust, and a focus on strategy. What had seemed like a perfect partnership over the phone turned into a relentless tug-of-war, each of us pulling in opposite directions.

But walking away didn't seem like an option. I had left behind a stable pharmaceutical sales job for this. We had sold our home. I had invested our savings, believing in the vision we had built together. To admit I had made a mistake? That felt like an impossible pill to swallow.

As the days passed, the differences between us only widened. What started as minor tensions grew into a gaping divide, stretching from an inconvenient gap to an unbridgeable chasm. Our values clashed; more significantly than that, they were misaligned. The tension seeped into every interaction, turning routine conversations into battles. I resented him, and it was clear that he felt the same about me. The stress followed me everywhere, creeping into my thoughts long after the workday ended. My relationships suffered, my health declined, and the business I had once been so excited about now felt like a trap I couldn't escape.

Introspection

Did fear ever keep you chained to a failing situation, when you were too scared to acknowledge the truth? What kept you there?

I knew within a few months that I had made a devastating mistake. The business wasn't the right fit, my family wasn't thriving, and no amount of stubbornness was going to change that.

One night after another tense conversation about the entire situation, I sat down with my wife and said what we had both been avoiding.

"We have to leave."

She didn't argue. She didn't tell me to try harder. She nodded, because she already knew. That moment, saying it out loud, hearing the words land, was the beginning of our way back.

We had no backup plan, but we knew staying would only dig the hole deeper. We got to work. My wife was on board and enthusiastic about getting back to West Virginia. She started reaching out to close friends, asking for help. I reached out to old colleagues, hoping I hadn't burned too many bridges when I left.

It wasn't instant, and it wasn't easy. We decided to sink no more. No more justifying. No more throwing good money and energy into something that would never work.

By the time we left Florida, our finances were in ruins. We had wiped out the significant savings we had built to fund the move. All we had left was $300 in our checking account. The financial security we had once taken for granted had vanished.

When we landed back in West Virginia, despite the financial devastation, we knew we weren't running away from failure—we were running toward what fit. We had lost almost everything, but what we gained was more valuable: the understanding that success isn't about financial stability but about making the right choices for the life you want.

A glimmer of hope came on a gray Tuesday morning shortly after our return to Morgantown. I had sent out another batch of résumés the night before. That morning an email popped up from a hiring manager I hadn't expected to hear from. It wasn't a job offer but a simple note saying, "Let's talk this week." That single line renewed my hope. It wasn't dramatic, but it was something. A reason to sit up straighter. A thread to follow.

That discussion eventually led to a job offer, and I returned to the pharmaceutical industry—not because I felt "called" to it but because life had nudged me back through a series of circumstances. I had trained in this field, and though I hadn't always appreciated it, losing it for a while had shifted my perspective. The detour was painful, but it deepened my gratitude for the work I had the opportunity to do. I was thrilled to go back to it.

Regaining my confidence didn't happen overnight. It took time to rebuild, to get my feet back under me, and to stop cringing every time I thought about the entire Florida ordeal. Over time, the experience stopped feeling like a complete disaster. Instead, it became proof that I could survive a setback, take the lesson, and move forward.

We all have our "Florida moments" when we bet big and lose, when we feel that we've blown it. But what if we stopped seeing those moments as proof of failure and instead as proof of growth, resilience, and clarity?

Because when I step back and look, that Florida disaster isn't a flop track on my life's album. It's one of the most important songs, the one that, years later, still teaches me something every time I hear it.

Your Brain Is a Terrible DJ

We all love a good success story. Real life doesn't always work like that. Real life is like most albums, in which the hits and the flops play on shuffle and no one's quite sure what's coming next.

The funny thing is, when we look at other people we see their highlight reels. Their wins seem obvious; their paths look clear. When we look at ourselves, every success feels debatable while every mistake feels permanent. We treat the good stuff as if it matters only when it's flawless, while engraving the bad stuff in permanent marker.

This again is what imposter syndrome does. It convinces us we're only as good as our worst moments, that every success was luck, that every failure is proof we don't belong. It's why we can recall, in excruciating detail, the time we blanked during an important meeting or sent an email with an embarrassing typo but struggle to remember the moments when we nailed it. Our mistakes play on repeat, while our wins don't make the set list.

I used to believe that my missteps, the awkward career pivots, the awful calls, the Florida disaster, and the terrible physician training were the only things that mattered. Now when I step back, I see my wins and my losses are part of the same picture. I can't erase the parts I don't like without losing the full story.

Maybe that's the whole point. Success isn't about collecting perfect moments. It's about seeing the messy, complicated, beautiful truth of the full album. Then letting yourself turn up the volume on the good stuff.

Failing Up (and Other Things I Didn't Plan On)

There's a reason people love comeback stories. We don't remember Steve Jobs for being forced out of the very company he started. He's remembered for turning Apple into one of the most influential brands in the world. We don't talk about Walt Disney being fired from a newspaper job because he "lacked imagination." He's remembered for building an empire of imagination that still shapes childhoods today. And Oprah? She was once told she wasn't fit for television. She's remembered for becoming one of the most powerful and trusted voices in media. I used to love stories like these. They made failure seem like a necessary step, proof that success was waiting on the other side. When it was my failure staring me in the face, I didn't feel that I was in the middle of some inspiring comeback story—I felt stuck.

For a long time the Florida business failure felt like a flashing neon sign that read, *See? You are not one of those people who will experience great success. Accept what life has given you and go sit in the corner.* It didn't matter that I had built a strong career before that. It didn't matter that I had picked myself up afterward. In my mind, that one failure was the truest thing about me. It was the anchor dragging behind me, the thing I thought everyone else could see.

It didn't matter that I had made bold choices, pushed through obstacles, and built a life that should have been proof of my resilience. My brain wasn't interested in the full picture. Instead, it zoomed in on every setback, every mistake, every moment when I didn't measure up. It was like standing in front of a wall covered with achievements but focusing only on the one crooked frame.

I wish I could say I had a defining cinematic moment where I realized failure wasn't the enemy. There wasn't one. It was more of a slow, uncomfortable realization, like breaking in a pair of shoes that pinch at first but eventually fit. The Florida failure changed me. It was a turning point that helped me understand myself in a way success never had.

That season of my life forced me to ask hard questions: *What do I want? What kind of work energizes me instead of draining me? What matters more—financial success or professional alignment?* I don't think I would have confronted those questions if everything had worked out the way I had planned.

That's the thing about failure. It's not always a door slamming shut. Sometimes it's a redirection. We think it's the end when it's the part of the story in which things get interesting.

It's easy to celebrate our wins. It's harder to appreciate our losses. But when I step back, I can see that the times I've struggled the most have also been the times I've grown the most. Maybe that's why comeback stories resonate with us. Deep down, we want to believe that failure isn't final.

It isn't.

The only way failure gets the last word is if you stop telling the story.

Reframing failure isn't something that happens overnight. Learning to see both the wins and the setbacks as part of the same journey takes practice. One of the simplest ways to do that? Start tracking them.

Introspection

What's one success you dismiss as 'luck'? What would it take for you to own that accomplishment?

How to Track Your Wins (Without Feeling like a Narcissist)

For the next few weeks, keep a "Greatest Hits & Misses" journal. At the end of each week, write one win and one miss (big or small). Maybe your win is that you crushed a work project or you made it through Monday without threatening to fight your printer. Maybe your miss is that you blanked in a meeting or that you accidentally replied "Thanks, you too" when the cashier told you to enjoy your meal. Whatever it is, write it down.

Then, for each one, answer these two questions:

- What made this moment happen? (For wins: What contributed to your success? For misses: What got in the way?)
- What did I learn from this?

That's it. No over-analyzing, no beating yourself up, no rewriting history. A simple way to remind yourself that your successes aren't flukes and your failures aren't fatal.

Over time you'll notice something: Your failures are never fatal. They are learning moments, redirections, or proof that you're human. Your successes? They aren't accidents. You played a role in making them happen.

The goal of this isn't to obsess over every detail of your life like a sports commentator breaking down game footage. It's training to see the full picture, the one in which your wins and losses coexist, not cancel each other out.

In the end, you're not your greatest hits. You're not your biggest misses. You're the full album.

It's a pretty good album.

As you go through this process, something powerful happens. You see your full story—not only the highlight reel, not only the missteps, but the entire picture.

It took me a long time to realize that self-worth isn't about erasing failures. It's about learning to see the full picture. The Florida business failure? For years I thought it was a permanent stain, a defining moment of incompetence. But when I zoom out, I see something different. I see a person who took a risk, learned what mattered to him, and came out the other side with clarity he didn't have before.

We allow complexity in others. We accept that our friends, our mentors, and our heroes have made mistakes, taken wrong turns, and figured things out along the way. For ourselves, we expect perfection.

That's not how this works. That's not how *any* of this works.

The good and the bad, the wins and the misses, the things you would brag about and the things you would rather bury—they all belong to you. They don't compete with each other. They complete each other.

In *A River Runs Through It* Norman Maclean struggles to understand his brother, Paul—a man full of contradictions, both troubled and extraordinary. In the end, all he can say is, "If you push me far enough, all I really know is that he was a fine fisherman." But his father corrects him: "You know more than that. He was beautiful."

I think about that moment a lot. Because isn't that all any of us want? To be seen as the whole of who we are, not as our failures or as our highlights, but as something more? And what if we saw ourselves as a complete and beautiful person? What change would that make in your thought life?

Maybe it's time to stop seeing yourself as a collection of mistakes and start seeing yourself as a whole person—one who has failed, yes, but also one who has achieved, grown, learned, and kept going, one who, despite everything, is still here, still trying, still showing up.

CHAPTER 10

Nobody Is Thinking about You
(and That's a Good Thing)

My grandmother had an uncanny ability to turn the smallest imperfection into a full-blown crisis. A single stray hair could derail her entire day. She stood in front of the mirror, coaxing, spraying, and rearranging, certain that one rebellious strand could draw the world's judgment.

"Grandma," I said one day, watching her do battle with a rogue curl, "nobody cares about your hair."

She shot me a look of pure disbelief. So I clarified: "Because they're all too busy worrying about their own hair."

She remained unconvinced, allowing her hair to throw her into bouts of unexplainable depression. She had grown up on an apple orchard in the post-Depression era. Her family was literally dirt poor. I can only imagine how that level of poverty would exacerbate self-consciousness. But you don't need to grow up on an orchard in the 1930s to know what that feels like. Countless others share this kind of thinking. Most of us have spent far too much time obsessing over something trivial—an awkward comment, a bad outfit choice, a misstep at work—convinced that everyone around us is cataloging our failures. Whether it's realizing your shirt's been inside out all day, calling a colleague by the wrong name in front of the entire team, or sharing your screen with seventeen open tabs you wish no one had seen, the fear is the same. We replay these moments in our heads, imagining a room full of people whispering about our mistakes—when nobody remembers.

Yet my grandmother held firm in her belief that every hair out of place was a scandal waiting to happen. As she got older and her health began failing, her obsession with her hair only intensified. Aging wasn't cooperating with her lifelong battle for follicular perfection.

So in what she believed was a brilliant solution, she took to covering it up. She wore headscarves and bandanas, tied and adjusted with precision, convinced this would keep people from noticing her bad hair days.

Except now, instead of blending in, she stood out more than ever. No one had ever paid attention to her hair before, but now people were noticing the scarves, asking about them, wondering if she had taken up a new fashion statement or was perhaps going through a phase as a backup singer for a '60s folk band. The very thing she had tried to hide had become a conversation starter.

It was another classic catch-22, a problem of her own creation. Her attempt to avoid scrutiny had only drawn more attention.

We convince ourselves that our minor flaws and awkward moments are under a microscope, so we overcorrect, overthink, and try controlling what people see. In doing so, we sometimes make things worse.

The world isn't watching us as closely as we think. The things we try to hide are often things nobody would have noticed in the first place.

My grandmother never quite believed me when I told her that no one was analyzing her hair. Maybe you will. Once you realize the spotlight you think is shining on you is in your head, you can stop performing and start living.

The Spotlight Effect

In college I once walked into class wearing a brand-new shirt, feeling confident about my style choices—until I looked down and saw the glaring evidence of my breakfast, a massive coffee stain right in the center. For the next hour I felt the stain command everyone's attention in the room. I imagined them whispering, smirking, maybe planning a campus-wide intervention to discuss my lack of coordination.

You know what happened? Nothing. No one said a word. No one glanced at me funny. Either they didn't notice or they had more important things to think about, like their own coffee stains, metaphorical or otherwise.

This is a perfect example of something psychologists call the "spotlight effect." It's the tendency to believe people are paying more attention to us than they are. It's the reason we agonize over minor mistakes, over-analyze our outfits, and replay awkward conversations in our heads as if they're the defining moments of our lives.

Most people are too self-absorbed to notice, much less remember, whatever we're obsessing over. Science proves how little others notice us.

Ask Barry Manilow.

In the early 2000s researchers Thomas Gilovich, Victoria Medvec, and Kenneth Savitsky conducted a study to test how much people overestimate how closely others are paying attention to them. They asked participants to wear an embarrassing T-shirt featuring Barry Manilow's face (a choice that, depending on your opinion of Barry, was humiliating or a flex).

After walking into a room full of strangers, researchers asked participants to estimate how many people noticed and remembered the shirt. The participants assumed at least half the room had clocked their questionable fashion statement.

The reality? Only twenty percent of people noticed it at all.

Engrossed in their own worlds, they were oblivious to the walking Barry Manilow billboard.

And if people don't notice something as obvious as a T-shirt with a celebrity's face plastered across it, they surely aren't noticing that typo you made in an email, the awkward joke you told at a party, or the way you mispronounced *Worcestershire* at dinner.

Introspection

Think about the last time you worried about a minor mistake you made. How long did you fixate on it? Now ask yourself, How long do I remember similar mistakes from other people?

The Barry Manilow study might be famous, but the spotlight effect plays out in our daily lives all the time.

- You trip on the sidewalk and look around, convinced that the universe saw you wipe out. The truth? The only person who noticed it was the guy delivering packages, and he already forgot because he was running late.
- You make a presentation at work and stumble over a sentence, assuming it ruined your credibility forever. Meanwhile, your coworkers were too busy thinking about what they were going to say next.
- You send a text with a minor typo and brace for judgment. The person on the other end skimmed it before responding with "Sounds good."
- You walk into a party wearing the wrong shoes and assume everyone is critiquing you. Most people stay too distracted, wondering if their zippers are down, to care.
- While performing for a live audience, you hit the wrong chord but keep your timing moving along. No one notices because they do not know the details of the song the way you do. All they know is the melody, and you kept that rolling.

It's an easy lesson to grasp. Most people are thinking about themselves, not you.

That might sound harsh, but it's not. It's freeing. You don't have to keep replaying that one embarrassing moment from five years ago. No one is holding onto the time you blanked in a meeting. While you're caught up worrying about how you come across, everyone else is too busy doing the same thing. So—relax.

What about That One Person Who Does Judge You?

Now, you might think, *Sure, most people don't care—but what about the one person who does?* The person who notices the mistake, who makes the comment, who seems to keep track of your flaws, as if it's his or her full-time job?

It's true. Occasionally there is that one person. I like to refer to them as jerks and with other less family-friendly adjectives. Maybe the jerk is a coworker who loves pointing out errors. Maybe it's a relative who has a photographic memory for every embarrassing thing you've ever done. Maybe it's a stranger on the Internet who had a little too much free time that day.

But here's the real question: Why do we let one person take up so much space in our minds?

You could receive ninety-nine compliments, but if one person makes a snide remark, that's the voice that lingers. You could have an entire room full of people enjoying the pottery you spent hours creating, but if one person looks unimpressed, that's the moment you replay in your head. Our brains treat life like Yelp, ignoring ninety-nine five-star reviews to fixate on the one complaint about slow service.

I once received a backhanded comment from someone about my work and spent hours stewing over it, turning it over in my head, analyzing it from every angle, and wondering if maybe the person was right. Then it hit me. This wasn't someone I respected. I wouldn't have gone to that person for advice. I wouldn't have asked for the person's opinion. Somehow, I had given this person a VIP seat in my brain, as if the person's words carried more weight than all the people who had encouraged me.

We do this all the time. We hand over the microphone to the person who criticizes us the most instead of the people who support us. It's like being at a party in which everyone is having a great time but you decide to spend the entire night focusing on the one person who looks bored.

The next time you catch yourself fixating on that one negative voice, ask yourself, *Does this person deserve this much of my time? Is he or she the person whose opinion should shape my decisions?* If not, let the person go. Evict the jerk.

It does go deeper. That one critic isn't thinking about you as much as you think. The critic made his or her comment and moved on. Maybe it wasn't about you. Maybe the person was having a bad day. Meanwhile, you're carrying it around as if it's written in stone.

You don't have to let that one person's opinion live rent-free in your mind. Show the person the door, take back the microphone, and move on with your life.

Introspection

Have you ever replayed an awkward moment for days, only to realize that no one else remembered it?

Why We Keep Falling for the Spotlight Effect

You would think the knowledge that people aren't staring at our every flaw would be enough to free us, but nope. Our brains, ever the drama queens, still insist on imagining an audience. There are a few reasons we fall into this trap again and again, and psychologists have narrowed it down to three main ones . . .

We Are the Stars of Our Own Movies

From the moment we wake up, our entire day plays out from our own perspective. We see our lives as one continuous film. We are the main character, the director, and the audience all at once. Because we are aware of our own thoughts, feelings, and actions, we assume everyone else is just as tuned in.

But everyone else is starring in their own movies. They're focused on their own worries, their own insecurities, and their own endless mental to-do lists. You might feel you're walking around with a spotlight on you, but most people are too distracted by their own scripts to pay attention to yours.

Think about it. If you accidentally wave at a stranger you thought you knew but really don't, it feels like a major event in your movie. To someone else? To that stranger? It's a three-second background shot before the camera cuts back to his or her storyline.

Our Brains Are Hardwired for Negativity

The human brain is like a hoarder of embarrassing memories. It collects them, stores them, and pulls them out at the worst imaginable times, like right before you fall asleep. Meanwhile, all the times you did something well? Those get shoved into the back of the attic, collecting dust.

This happens because of the negativity bias. Our brains focus more on negative experiences than on positive ones. From an evolutionary standpoint, this makes sense. Back when survival depended on avoiding danger, remembering terrible experiences was crucial. If you ate a weird-looking berry and got sick, your brain made sure you never forgot that berry's shape, color, and exact location.

The problem is that our brains still use this same system in a modern world, where "threats" are a lot less life-or-death. Instead of avoiding poisonous berries, we fixate on that awkward thing we said in a meeting three years ago. Instead of replaying moments of success, we replay the one time we tripped in front of a group of people.

Because we assume others are keeping track of our mistakes as much as we are, we convince ourselves that everyone remembers. They don't.

Everyone Else Is Just as Self-Absorbed as You Are

If you need proof that people aren't watching you as closely as you think, take a moment to flip the perspective.

- How much time do you spend analyzing other people's minor mistakes?
- Have you ever seen someone stumble over his or her words and thought about it for more than five seconds? No.
- Have you ever witnessed someone forgetting to zip his or her fly and replayed it in your head for days? Doubtful.
- Have you ever sat in a meeting, laser-focused on someone else's ringing cell phone he or she forgot to silence, rather than worrying about how you were going to contribute to the conversation at hand? Almost certainly not.

Most of us are walking around so caught up in our own thoughts that we ignore other people's small blunders. We assume all the others are keeping score on us when they're too busy keeping score on themselves.

Why This Matters
Understanding why we fall for the spotlight effect is the first step in breaking free from it. When you realize that most people are too busy starring in their own movies to notice yours, that your brain is exaggerating the importance of your mistakes, and that nobody else is holding onto your awkward moments as you are, you gain a huge amount of freedom.

- You can stop over-analyzing.
- You can stop worrying about what you wore to that event.
- You can relax, knowing that whatever you're fixating on, everyone else has already moved on from.

The next time you catch yourself cringing over something you said or did, ask yourself this: *If someone else did the same thing, would you still be thinking about it a week later?* If not, then there's no need to worry.

How to Break Free from the Spotlight Effect

Knowing that most people aren't scrutinizing your every move is helpful, but that doesn't mean the fear of looking foolish disappears. When we understand our mistakes aren't as memorable as we think, it's still hard to shake that little voice in our head whispering, *Yeah, but what if they do remember?*

The key is learning how to shift your mindset in the moment. When self-consciousness kicks in, these strategies can help you break free from the spotlight effect and move on faster.

The Five-Second Rule

Here's a simple trick: Anytime you catch yourself obsessing over something embarrassing, flip the script. Ask yourself, *if someone else did this, would I still be thinking about it five seconds later?*

If the answer is no, that's a good sign that you're holding onto something nobody else noticed or cared about.

Think about the last time you saw someone trying to exit through a door that needs to be pushed open instead of pulled. The person struggled with the pulling motion twice and then figured out that pushing is the key. It's funny for a second but gone just as quickly. Your brain moved on to something else, like what to eat for dinner. The same thing happens when you make a slight mistake. People notice—then they forget.

And if they *don't* forget? That's their problem—not yours.

Move on as They Do

If you're worried that someone noticed your awkward moment, take a second to picture that same person making a similar mistake. *Would you hold on to it? Would you bring it up a week later? Or would you move on with your life?*

Most of the time we don't judge others as harshly as we judge ourselves. If you wouldn't hold someone else's minor mistake against the person, why assume he or she is holding yours against you?

Imagine you're in a meeting and a coworker laughs too loud at a statement that wasn't supposed to be funny. Would you spend the rest of the day replaying it in your head, analyzing what it meant about the person's intelligence or competence? Of course not. You would forget about it almost immediately. So why assume that when you stumble, everyone else is treating it like breaking news?

Everyone's Thinking about His or Her Own Hair

As noted earlier, my grandmother believed the world was evaluating her appearance. No matter how much I reassured her that nobody was paying attention to her hair, she refused to believe me. We're all too preoccupied with our own "bad hair days" to notice anyone else's.

It doesn't matter whether the worry is about appearance, performance, or social blunders; we all spend more time thinking about ourselves than about each other.

Next time you feel self-conscious, remind yourself that people are too busy worrying about their own flaws to focus on yours. If they notice at all, they'll forget by lunchtime.

The Zoom-Out Perspective

When you're caught in an overthinking spiral, zoom out. Imagine yourself five years from now. Will you still be losing sleep over that awkward joke, that mispronounced word, or the time you tripped walking up the stairs?

If the answer is no, then why waste time stressing about it now?

Think back to an embarrassing moment from five years ago. Does it still sting, or does it seem ridiculous that you ever worried about it? If something doesn't feel important in hindsight, chances are that it's not that important now.

The Famous Fall for It Too

If you still doubt people pay less attention to you than you think, consider how the world's most accomplished figures have struggled with the same illusion. These are people who have stood under actual spotlights, had their words analyzed, and seen their names in headlines—yet they believed others were judging them more harshly than reality suggested. Despite their success, they assumed every flaw, every misstep, every moment of doubt was being noticed and remembered. Here's what separates them: They learned to push forward anyway.

Take Stephen King, an author whose books have sold over 350 million copies. You might assume someone that successful would move through life with unwavering confidence. King has spoken about how self-doubt almost kept him from publishing *Carrie*, the novel that launched his career. He assumed no one would want to read it, that it wasn't worth finishing. He tossed the manuscript into the trash. His wife, Tabitha, pulled it out and urged him to keep going. The book defined modern horror fiction. Now, after decades of bestsellers, King still wonders whether each new book will measure up.

No one sat around dissecting his every word, waiting to declare him a fraud. Readers didn't scrutinize him the way he feared; they wanted a great story. The judgment he worried about existed only in his mind.

Frida Kahlo fell into the same trap. Today she is one of the most recognized artists in the world, but during her lifetime she believed people saw her only as Diego Rivera's wife. She assumed her paintings wouldn't stand on their own, that they weren't worth serious consideration. While she worried about being overlooked, her work captivated others. Critics and collectors didn't see her as an afterthought. They saw something new, something powerful. Now her name eclipses Rivera's in cultural significance. The art she once doubted became the art that defined her.

Those who have led nations aren't immune to this illusion. Barack Obama, a two-term U.S. president, has admitted to questioning whether he belonged in the rooms he walked into. Early in his career he dreaded the moment someone would pull him aside and expose him as a mistake. He assumed others were scrutinizing his every move, waiting to expose his shortcomings. Were they? Or was everyone in that room focused on his or her own responsibilities, too preoccupied to dissect every detail of his presence?

The surrounding people weren't spending their time picking apart his qualifications. They were listening to what he had to say, assessing the value he brought. He assumed he was under a microscope, but no one was holding it.

Then there's Amy Poehler, a woman who built an entire career on confidence and quick thinking. If anyone should feel at home in the spotlight, it's her. Yet in her memoir *Yes Please* she describes how imposter syndrome never faded as her fame grew. Inadequacy lingered as she progressed from improv stages to *Saturday Night Live* to Hollywood. Instead of obsessing over whether she measured up, she focused on the work in front of her. She didn't waste time wondering whether people were questioning her talent. She kept creating.

That's the difference.

Stephen King assumed no one would care about his work, but the world wasn't waiting to reject him—it was waiting to read him. Frida Kahlo feared being dismissed, yet her art mesmerized people. Barack Obama entered rooms expecting judgment, but most people focused too much on their own priorities to analyze his every move. Amy Poehler worried that self-doubt meant she didn't belong, but instead of letting that thought control her, she did the thing anyway.

We fall into this same trap every day, replaying awkward moments and believing others noticed every misstep. We convince ourselves that people are scrutinizing our mistakes, filing them away for future judgment. How much time do *you* spend cataloging other people's minor blunders? How many times have you memorized someone else's stumbles in a meeting or the way he or she mispronounced a word? You haven't. Your focus, like everyone else's, is on your own life.

The world isn't keeping score on you. Most people are too busy thinking about their own challenges, their own insecurities, their own fears to analyze yours. When they do notice something about you, they aren't carrying it around in their minds as you are.

If a bestselling author, a world-renowned artist, a U.S. president, and a comedy icon have all overestimated how much others were watching them, what are the chances that your coworkers, your friends, or the random stranger at the grocery store is still thinking about that awkward thing you said last week?

The difference between these successful people and everyone else isn't that they never felt self-doubt—it's that they didn't let it stop them. They realized that the judgment they feared existed only in their own heads.

If history's most accomplished people have fallen for the illusion that others were watching and keeping score, then maybe it's time we stop believing it too.

What This Means for You

If you had a list of every time you worried about what people thought of you, it would be long. The list of what people actually remember? Almost blank.

We assume every mistake, awkward moment, or misstep is being recorded somewhere, as if there's an invisible panel of judges tallying up our flaws. Most people are too busy playing the star athlete in their own games to pay attention to the score in your game.

What do you do with this information?

First, let it remind you that self-doubt doesn't disappear because you accomplish something. You don't wake up one day, look in the mirror, and feel you belong. If the most brilliant and successful people in the world still feel that they aren't enough sometimes, maybe the goal isn't to eliminate imposter syndrome. Maybe it's learning how to manage it and keep moving forward anyway.

Second, stop letting the fear of judgment keep you from showing up. The people who do great things aren't the ones who never doubt themselves—they're the ones who refuse to let it hold them back.

The next time you obsess over whether people noticed something embarrassing about you, ask yourself, *Would it stop Stephen King from writing? Would it stop Frida Kahlo from painting? Would it stop Amy Poehler from getting up on stage and making people laugh?* No, and it shouldn't stop you either—because the only person keeping track of your mistakes is you. Once you let go of that, you're free—free to show up, take risks, and live your life without worrying about an audience that isn't watching.

Life Is Too Short to Live under Imaginary Scrutiny

The story of my grandmother, shared earlier, makes me ache because her fear kept her from living.

There were dinners she declined because she didn't like how her hair looked, parties she skipped because she couldn't make it cooperate, church services where she sat rigid and distracted, tugging at her scarf instead of singing the hymns she loved. To her, every gathering was an audience waiting to catch her at her worst. In reality, no one noticed. Nobody was analyzing her hair. They were too busy thinking about their own worries, their own insecurities, their own metaphorical stray strands.

She spent so much time under imaginary scrutiny that she missed opportunities for joy. And as I noted before, she never fully believed me when I told her that nobody cared as much as she thought.

Most of us do the same thing with different "scarves." Maybe it's the presentation we don't give because we're afraid of messing up one slide. Maybe it's the job we don't apply for because we assume people will laugh at our résumé. Maybe it's the photo we don't post because we're convinced someone will zoom in and notice a flaw. We tell ourselves it's safer to hide than to risk being judged—but hiding comes at its own cost.

Imaginary scrutiny can steal from us more effectively than real criticism ever could. A cutting remark might sting for a day, but our own self-doubt can lock us away for years.

Think about what you've already missed because of it. Did you say no to an invitation because you didn't feel confident in how you looked? Did you hold back an idea in a meeting because you worried someone would think it was silly? Did you stop yourself from starting a project because you assumed people would question why you tried? Each time we let the imaginary spotlight dictate our choices, we shrink a little. We trade potential joy for momentary safety.

My grandmother's story is a cautionary tale, but it's also a reminder of what's possible if we let go. Imagine the freedom of showing up as you are, stray hairs and all. Imagine laughing at your own slip-ups instead of obsessing over them. Imagine walking into a room believing that most people are too tangled in their own lives to catalog yours.

Because that's the truth. Others aren't keeping score. Strangers aren't memorizing your stumbles. Friends aren't archiving your embarrassing moments for future use. That weight you feel pressing down on you? It's one you've placed there yourself. And if you placed it there, you can set it down.

If my grandmother had spent half as much time enjoying herself as she did fighting her reflection, she would have laughed more, traveled more, and said yes more often. She would have lived with less fear and more joy. She deserved that freedom. So do you.

Introspection

What would you do if you believed nobody was keeping score?
Would you take more risks? Would you be kinder to yourself?
Would you stop waiting for permission to enjoy your own life?

Life is far too short to waste time fixing what was never broken. The stray hair, the awkward joke, the forgotten name—none of these define you. What defines you is how fully you show up in the moments that matter.

So go ahead. Wear the outfit. Share the idea. Tell the story. Make the mistake. Laugh at yourself. Join the party. Step into the picture. The spotlight was never as harsh as you imagined, and most of the audience isn't watching.

In the next section we'll dive into practical ways to take control of that inner monologue, quiet the voice of self-doubt, and start showing up as the real, confident you.

PART FOUR

LETTING YOURSELF IN

CHAPTER 11

Don't Believe Everything You Think

Your brain is a storyteller and a terrible one at that. It spins dramatic worst-case scenarios, blows small mistakes out of proportion, and somehow always casts you as the clueless fraud who's about to get exposed.

I know this because my brain has done it to me more times than I can count.

A while back I took up cycling—not casual weekend rides but serious, spandex-clad, suffer-fest cycling. At first I rode solo, getting a feel for my new road bike and pushing myself at my own pace. Falling off a slow-moving bike while I learned to clip in and out of the pedals was something I wanted to do without an audience. Once I had the basics down, I joined a group ride. These weren't weekend warriors. These were fast guys, the kind who had been riding for years, their legs carved from granite, their lungs conditioned to laugh in the face of steep climbs.

My brain took one look at them and launched into full-blown disaster mode.

You're going to get dropped in the first five miles.
You'll be the guy everyone has to wait for.
They'll roll their eyes, annoyed that some rookie is slowing them down.
You'll crash. Or puke. Or both.

By the time I clipped into my pedals for my first group ride, my brain had already decided my fate. I was going to be dropped within minutes, left gasping on the side of the road while the real cyclists disappeared over the horizon. They would be shaking their heads in disappointment, wondering why I had showed up. Anxiety didn't just creep in—it consumed me. The entire disaster script played out in my mind, and I had no choice but to follow along.

Then something strange happened. Reality didn't follow the script. Nobody laughed when I struggled on a climb. Nobody sighed in frustration when I fell behind. Instead of getting dropped and humiliated, I was getting advice, real-time coaching from riders who had once been where I was. My brain convinced me I would fail this test. In reality? It was a learning experience—and a fun one at that.

I kept up. Sure, I got dropped on a couple of hills, but I did not end up gasping on the side of the road. Instead of sneers or eye rolls, the more experienced riders encouraged me. They told me that I was doing great for it being the first time. They offered tips on pacing and drafting; they helped me improve. Instead of waiting for me, they pulled me forward.

It was nothing like the story I had told myself before the ride. My brain had written an entire fictional disaster movie, and not a single scene had happened. In fact, a whole different movie played out. I thought I was buying a ticket to *The Exorcist* and ended up watching *Rocky*. They welcomed me into their group and I learned something new.

That ride taught me how often my brain writes complete fiction. My brain isn't a talented writer. It's not churning out Oscar-winning screenplays. It's a low-budget hack, recycling the same plots over and over. I stumble once, and it becomes *The Fall that Ended My Career*. I hesitate for a beat in a meeting, and it turns into *The Moment Everyone Realized I'm an Imposter*.

If you've ever sat through your own mental disaster movie, you know what I mean. Our minds spin stories with ourselves cast as the fool, the fraud, or the failure—because our brains are natural "catastrophizers."

We hear these stories and then absorb them. We let the imagined details harden into facts and the fiction preach like gospel. But a script in your head isn't the same as the truth.

Introspection

What else could be true besides the worst-case scenarios
in your head?

That's where the work begins. You don't have to silence the voice. That's impossible since it never shuts up. But you *can* rewrite the script. You can challenge the fiction, flip the scene, and choose a different ending.

When you do, you'll discover what I did on that ride: Reality is rarely the horror movie your brain promised. More often than not, it's a different film entirely, one in which you learn, grow, and maybe surprise yourself.

That's when the real story begins.

Bad Brain Movies

My brain has a whole production company dedicated to cranking out bad movies starring me as the incompetent lead. They're all straight-to-streaming, low-budget flicks with dramatic titles and terrible scripts that make me nauseous, sweaty, and insecure. The same titles get recycled over and over. Maybe you'll recognize a few:

- *I'm Not Ready*—Any time something new shows up, my brain insists I need ten more years of training.
- *I Got Lucky*—I succeed but my brain tells me it was a fluke.
- *I Don't Belong Here*—The classic fraud narrative; everyone else belongs, but I'm the imposter.

- *Everyone Else Has It Figured Out*—A crowd favorite in which I'm the only one stumbling while everyone else has the secret manual.
- *If I Were Good at This, It Would Be Easy*—Struggle equals proof I don't have what it takes.
- *I Have to Prove Myself Every Time*—Every success is a temporary hall pass I'll lose if I'm not perfect.

The scripts aren't original. They're tired reruns. And once you see them for what they are, it's easier to step in as the editor.

The disaster genre is a regular on my mind's marquee. Miss a single quarterly sales number after crushing every goal for the last three years? Cue the dramatic soundtrack and horrified faces as the screen flashes *The End of My Career: Part II*.

Leadership cares about my entire track record, not one blip. But in sales it's easy to forget that. We're trained to obsess over the next number, the next deal, the next leaderboard update. Most sales teams post rankings as if they're fantasy football, and we stare at them daily. If we're not number one, we feel like failures—which is absurd, because only one person *can* be number one. So the other hundred or so people are walking around convinced they're losing. Ricky Bobby's phrase "If you ain't first, you're last" from *Talladega Nights* lives rent-free in our psyches.

It's insanity, but my brain buys into it every time. The reality? The organization knows my history. They trust my value. No one is making sweeping judgments about what I did or didn't do in a single quarter. That's the awful movie in my head.

At other times it prefers soap operas. One awkward misstep becomes a multi-season storyline that everyone is still whispering about behind my back. My brain convinces me that it's part of company lore, that in Slack channels or group texts people are still chuckling about the thing I did months ago.

Remember the terrible physician training meeting I shared back in chapter 7? My brain certainly does. It still drags me back to the same physical embarrassment, complete with the sweaty palms, the hot face, the voice that wouldn't cooperate. Never mind that it happened at a completely different company with a completely different group of people. Nobody at my current job knows it happened. Yet my brain acts as if the old cast of characters has followed me to this new season, still huddled in the break room talking about it. And worse, some days I actually believe that.

And then there's the heist movie. This one shows up not when I mess up but when something goes right. I get an opportunity, an invitation, or a promotion, and my brain immediately cues the *Ocean's Eleven* soundtrack. Clearly, I didn't earn it. I slipped past security, and sooner or later someone will figure it out.

I can't tell you how many times this has hit me in the promotion process. I've had years of solid performance reviews, exceeded goals, and built solid connections, all the things you're supposed to do in a competitive environment. I get to the interview stage, which should feel like validation. Instead, my brain whispers, *You don't belong in a role like this.* And once that thought shows up, it leaks into everything: the way I phrase an answer, the confidence in my tone, and my body language.

Don't get me wrong. I'm proud of what I've accomplished. But I've also watched people with fewer qualifications and less experience slide past me, not because they were more capable but because they weren't weighed down by their own mental heist plot. While I was busy worrying that I had been let into the vault by mistake, they were already walking out with the job.

Sometimes the script takes a darker turn into conspiracy thriller territory. Someone gives me genuine praise, and my brain whispers, *They don't really mean it. They're being polite. Or worse, they're setting you up for the big reveal later: You don't belong here.* My brain turns encouragement into foreshadowing for a plot twist that never comes.

This happens in my musical life all the time. I'll play for an audience, and afterward someone offers a sincere compliment. Instead of letting it land, something deep inside me insists, *I've tricked them. I'm not a musician. I'm a hack.* If they heard Ben or Chris or Dave play, then they would know the truth. I don't deserve the praise.

The wild part is that these movies feel real while they're playing in my head. My palms sweat, my stomach knots, my heart races. The story doesn't read like fiction; it reads like a documentary. I don't watch the movie—I believe it. I buy the ticket, grab the popcorn, and settle in for another screening of *You Don't Belong Here.*

What I need to remember is that my brain is not Morgan Freeman narrating objective truth. It's more like a drunk sports commentator—overconfident, loud, and wrong about half the plays. When I finally pause long enough to ask, *Wait—is this happening, or is this my brain making up drama again?* the answer is almost always the latter.

The difference now is that I've learned how to hit the stop button. My brain still presses play on these ridiculous films, but I don't sit through the whole thing anymore. I can walk out halfway through instead of staying until the credits roll. Self-doubt still shows up, but it doesn't run the entire show the way it used to.

And that's the good news. Just because my brain writes the script doesn't mean I have to star in it. The movies will keep rolling but I get to decide whether I'm in the cast or walking out of the theater.

The real danger of these mental movies isn't how bad they feel in the moment. It's their ability to talk you out of taking risks in the first place. I was once asked to open a thirty-minute set for two incredible bands, the kind of musicians who commanded the stage as if they were born on it. My brain rolled the trailer for *The Hack Exposed,* starring me. The script was brutal: *You'll bomb. Everyone will see that you don't belong here. They'll wonder why you said yes to doing this.* Those lines looped on repeat for weeks before the gig until I was convinced that the ending was already written.

I showed up early to get comfortable with the stage. The first band was still doing their sound check, which was . . . let's say, different from mine. I was one guy with an acoustic guitar. They were five guys with drums, keys, bass, sax, vocals, youth, pectoral muscles busting through silk shirts, Chelsea boots, and a rock-star presence as natural as green grass in Ireland. They were melting faces during their *sound check.* It was like Sly and the Family

Stone, Hendrix, and Prince had formed a supergroup. My brain upgraded the disaster movie into 5K ultra HD.

When they finished, they couldn't have been nicer. They helped make space for my tiny setup among their wall of expensive gear. The sound guy dialed me in as best as he could. But my brain still screamed, *This is going to be a disaster!*

Thirty minutes later I took the stage. The first two songs weren't great. I stumbled, missed notes, and could feel the nerves buzzing through my fingers. But then something shifted. I thought, *Well, nothing you do next can be worse than those last two songs,* and I let go. The rest of the set came together. The songs landed. At one point I saw a few people dancing to my Sam Cooke-style originals. By the end, I was enjoying myself.

Afterward I sat back and enjoyed three hours of music from those amazing bands. At the end of the night, both groups told me how much they loved my set. Of course, my brain tried to dismiss it as politeness. But then a few audience members came up and said the same thing. Reality hadn't matched the disaster movie at all. It wasn't perfect. But it was real, and it was good.

That night reinforced the fact that my brain will always try to write the script, but reality gets the final cut. And while I can't stop the movies from starting, I've learned I can step in as the editor, cross out the worst lines, and give myself a different ending.

Quick Rewrites When Your Brain Goes Cinematic

- **The Horror Flick → The Training Montage.** Instead of "This will kill me," try "This is how I get stronger."
- **The Heist → The Invitation.** Instead of "I snuck in by mistake," try "I was let in because I bring something valuable."
- **The Soap Opera → The Comedy.** Instead of "Everyone is still whispering about my mistake," try "Most people forgot five minutes later."

- **The Disaster Movie → The Adventure Film.** Instead of "This is the end," try "This is where the story gets interesting."

Rewriting as Lived Experience

The rewrites don't happen on grand stages. They're not Oscar-worthy either. They happen in small, everyday moments to everyday people, the places where imposter thoughts sneak in and whisper their nonsense.

Take my friend who was unceremoniously shown the door during a "downsizing." On paper he was a rock star: He had played a pivotal role in helping one drug become best-in-class, holding three different roles across sales, operations, and marketing. He had deep insight into the entire landscape of that therapy.

There's an ugly truth in corporate life, though—relationships often matter more than performance. My friend valued real intellectual debate. He asked hard questions, applied scientific rigor to commercial decisions, and sometimes delivered news that powerful people didn't want to hear. And as anyone who has dealt with narcissistic leaders knows, dissenting facts can be a career hazard. Eventually he was shown the door.

It stung. He remembered the endless hours he had spent trying to stay one step ahead of those personalities. The stress bled into his marriage and his parenting. The bad brain movie was clear: *You're too difficult. You're not worth the trouble. You'll never get another good job.*

Then he rewrote the script. He reminded himself: *I'm an expert in three parts of the commercialization process. I have trusted relationships with key opinion leaders in this disease state. I know more about this market than the people interviewing me.* That shift changed how he walked into his interviews.

The result? Several offers. He chose a company launching a revolutionary therapy in the very disease area in which he already had credibility and connections. Months in, his new leadership team now seeks him out for advice because of the value he provides.

Same person. Same skills. Different script. That's the difference between living your story and living the one someone else wrote for you.

In music, talent doesn't always follow a straight path. Some musicians chase the charts. Others carve out their own lane, building work that may never fit neatly into a Top 40 box but is every bit as masterful.

My friend Ben Townsend chose the second path. He can play any stringed instrument, but the fiddle and banjo are where he shines. As a teenager he studied under some of West Virginia's old-time legends like Melvin Wine and Lester McCumbers. Their music runs through his veins.

The safe path for Ben would have been to stay there, keeping those traditions alive as they were handed to him. And he could have. People would have loved him for it. But Ben's influences go far beyond fiddle tunes. Before forming The Fox Hunt band, he was experimenting in math rock and metal. He's always carried multiple genres at once. People just happen to know him best for old-time.

Instead of ignoring those other parts of himself, he pulled them in. After The Fox Hunt broke up, he kept collaborating with hip-hop artists, metal projects, and electronic musicians. Most striking of all, he blended the old West Virginia tunes he had grown up on with dance beats and electronic rhythms, creating something that isn't techno and isn't fiddle. It's entirely his own.

And he hasn't stopped there. Ben runs a studio, mentors younger players, and raises funds for local musicians. His nontraditional path requires wearing many hats, but that's the point: He refuses to be boxed in.

It would have been easy for him to stay inside the script his peers expected. But he rewrote it. He leaned into his full identity and now creates music that reflects all of him: his roots, his quirks, his curiosity. The result is something brilliant, something that couldn't have existed if he had stayed inside the old script.

Parenting has its own special category of bad brain movies, and one of the most brutal is the milestone script. You know the one: *Your child isn't walking yet? Every other kid in the neighborhood is practically sprinting. Your toddler isn't stringing words together? The neighbor's kid is writing sonnets. That* voice creeps in at doctor visits, playground conversations, and especially in the scroll of social media where every parent seems to have a prodigy.

A friend of mine fell hard into this trap when her son wasn't hitting the "expected" speech milestones. She had read the books, listened to the podcasts, and absorbed every chart her pediatrician handed her. By the time her son turned two, her brain had the disaster film fully story boarded: *He'll never catch up. I failed him. Everyone will know I'm a bad mom.*

The anxiety wasn't abstract—it was physical as well. Her stomach tightened every time another parent mentioned his or her kid's growing vocabulary. She avoided playdates because she didn't want to sit in the circle of toddlers singing the alphabet while hers sat happily stacking blocks in silence.

Then she caught herself. She realized the "movie" she was watching wasn't reality. Her son was happy, curious, and engaged with the world. He was simply not interested in talking yet. And when she stepped back, she remembered her own brother had been a "late talker" who grew into the loudest, funniest guy in the room.

So she rewrote the script. Instead of *I've failed my son,* she started telling herself, *Every child has his or her own timeline. My job isn't to rush him—it's to support him.* That rewrite shifted everything. She leaned into his focus, his creativity, his patience with building elaborate towers. She celebrated his strengths instead of panicking over his silence.

Eventually his words started tumbling out. First a trickle, then a flood. And when they came, they came with the kind of confidence that made it clear he had been listening all along.

Same child. Same parent. Different script.

That's the lesson that milestones don't always teach: Kids grow at their own pace, and the scariest part of the movie is often the intermission.

What all these stories have in common (my friend in corporate life, Ben with his music, and my friend navigating parenting milestones) is that none of them changed who they were at the core. They didn't wake up with brand-new talents or personalities. They simply stopped living inside someone else's script. My corporate friend realized he wasn't the "difficult" employee his last company had painted him to be. Ben refused to shrink himself into a traditionalist box because that's what people expected of him. My friend with her son stopped measuring her parenting against other people's timelines. Same people. Same gifts. Same love. The difference was the stories they chose to believe.

That's the real power of rewriting: It doesn't erase the hard stuff. It doesn't silence the doubts forever. It opens a door into another way of seeing yourself, a door that says, *What if the movie in my head isn't the only version?*

Rewrites aren't limited to work, art, or parenting. They can happen at any stage of life. In Jonas Jonasson's *The 100-Year-Old Man Who Climbed Out the Window and Disappeared*, the main character, Allan Karlsson, is supposed to spend his 100th birthday in a nursing home. That's the script: Fade into the background, wait out your days. Instead, Allan climbs out the window and stumbles into a series of absurd adventures that defy every expectation of what "old age" should look like. The book is ridiculous at times, but it's also figuratively true: The script isn't finished until you decide it is.

What makes Allan so compelling is how he responds to the unexpected. When a suitcase full of cash lands in his hands, he doesn't panic. He shrugs, picks it up, and figures he'll see where it takes him. When a criminal gang comes after him, he treats it like a small, inconvenient detour. When bodies start piling up, he doesn't spiral into worst-case thinking. He accepts the moment, pours himself a vodka, and keeps moving.

The same pattern shows up in his backstory. As a young explosive expert during the war, he blew up the wrong thing more than once, but instead of being paralyzed by failure, he stepped into whatever came next. He worked with Franco, Truman, Stalin, and de Gaulle—all by accident, all because he had an almost radical ability to meet life where it was instead of where he thought it should be.

Allan is the opposite of a bad brain movie. He doesn't waste time writing disaster scripts in his head. He lives the scene he's in, lets the river carry him, and trusts that the next bend will sort itself out. It's absurdist comedy, yes, but also a reminder that sometimes the most powerful rewrite isn't a dramatic line change—it's choosing not to freak out when the story takes an unexpected turn.

That's the thread that ties them all together. Whether it's a seasoned professional who's told he's too much, a musician boxed in by genre, a parent convinced she's failing, or a fictional centenarian refusing to sit still—the common act is rewriting, choosing reality over fear, choosing curiosity over catastrophe, choosing to keep moving when the old script says to stop.

If your brain insists on writing bad movies, fine. Let it. Remember: You get to edit. You get to improvise. And when necessary, you can always climb out the window.

Let Yourself In

That's the gift of a rewrite is that you stop buying tickets to the worst-case film and let the real story roll. And make no mistake—your brain will keep pitching scripts. That's its full-time job. One moment it's a disaster movie, the next it's a soap opera, and before long you're starring in a conspiracy thriller about how everyone thinks you're a fraud. Fine. Let the brain churn them out. Remember: You don't have to star in every one.

That's where rewriting comes in. A single line swap can shift the entire plot. *I don't belong* becomes *I'm here to learn.* Then the story shifts from courtroom drama to training montage. You can change the tone with a lighter voice, like a coach urging you forward on a climb or a friend telling you it's okay to stumble through the first two songs before you find your groove. If you don't like the script, don't recite it. Cross out the bad lines. Step out of the theater halfway through. Or, of course, when all else fails—climb out the window.

Which brings us back to Allan Karlsson, the centenarian who decided the story handed to him wasn't the story he wanted. On paper his part was written: Sit quietly in a nursing home and wait for the credits to roll. Instead, he wrote his own twist. He climbed out the window, stepped into the unknown, and proved that a script has power only if you agree to play along.

Allan isn't a model of careful planning or flawless decision-making. He's a caricature of something more useful: the freedom that comes when you stop treating the "official" storyline as mandatory. His adventures are outrageous, but the lesson is simple. At any stage (whether you're 20, 40, or 100) you can decide that the plot isn't finished. You can set down the script in your hands and improvise a new one.

That's what rewrites are really about. They don't erase self-doubt or tie everything up in a neat bow. They keep you from mistaking the bad brain movie for the only version of reality. Every rewrite is a way of saying, *The story isn't finished until I decide it is.*

So often we live in disbelief: *I can't believe they let me in.* We whisper it after promotions, relationships, opportunities, as if some cosmic mix-up landed us in the wrong room.

But the deeper rewrite is this: No one else has to let you in. You get to let yourself in.

That's the line.

You always belonged in the room, the meeting, the group ride, the stage, the story.

Rewriting is the beginning. The payoff comes when you *live* that rewrite, when you ride with the group anyway, raise your hand in the meeting, sing the next song, or parent the kid in front of you instead of the one in your head.

Next we'll talk about how to own the room (and your life) when the old script still tries to drag you offstage.

Introspection

What would letting yourself in look like today? What is the one small step you need to take?

CHAPTER 12

Own the Room
(Even When You Don't Feel like It)

Before *Hamilton* ever hit Broadway, Lin-Manuel Miranda stood at a mic in the White House with one song and a stomach full of doubt. He had already created *In the Heights*, a Tony-winning hip-hop/Latin musical about Washington Heights, but he still wondered whether a hip-hop show about Alexander Hamilton would land or fizzle.

He performed anyway.

That's the point. Confidence isn't the disappearance of fear—confidence is showing up even while fear rides shotgun.

For years I treated confidence like a personality trait that some people had and some didn't. Turns out it's closer to *presence*. Presence is how you enter a room, take a seat, use your voice, and stay in the moment while your brain whispers that you don't belong.

This chapter is about doing that on purpose, not faking it, not waiting to feel ready—acting as though you belong on a stage, in a boardroom, in whatever room your life asks you to step into.

People who seem confident aren't fearless, but they've learned habits that let them move with fear in the room: starting strong, steadying their breaths, holding eye contact, slowing the rush in their voices, recovering after stumbles, and keeping on. The good news: Those habits are learnable.

Miranda didn't know if *Hamilton* would work when he sang that first number. He treated the moment as if it belonged to him and stepped in. That's the move we're after—not certainty about the outcome but the choice to show up, take part, and claim your place.

You Don't Have to Feel Ready to Look Ready

Several years ago a friend of mine jumped from product manager to vice president of marketing at a large pharma company. I knew her from a previous gig. She was sharp then. Now she was leading the show.

If you've never been to a pharma sales meeting, picture a Disney World production with badges: main-stage lights, hype videos, breakouts stacked back to back, and side conversations in every hallway where you're expected to say the right things to the right people in under thirty seconds. As VP she was under the microscope. In all leadership positions, but especially in VP leadership positions, everything you do is exaggerated. My friend had to provide guidance and motivation while trying to appear as if she did not have any flaws. Yes, it's an impossible standard.

She had a sixty-minute main-stage slot: the marketing update. A thousand people. Teleprompter, timer, confidence monitor, and all the rest of the works. From the outside she looked bulletproof.

She slid into the chair next to me before they introduced her to the main stage. I told her how steady she had seemed all week. She smiled. "Want a secret?" she asked me. I nodded. "I've been scared out of my mind." Then she showed me what she had in her hand: an index card with three anchors:

- **First line:** "Good morning—here's our goal for the next hour."
- **Three-bullet spine:** where we are, what we're deciding, what I need from you.
- **Last line:** "If you remember one thing, remember this . . ."

She wasn't waiting until she felt ready. She had a plan for looking ready.

When they introduced her, she planted her feet, dropped her shoulders, and took two slow breaths. She started with the first sentence, a touch louder than normal, then settled into her natural voice. She picked one friendly face in the third row as her anchor and let sentences end instead of racing to fill silence.

Ten minutes in, the slide froze. No panic. She took a sip of water. "Give me ten seconds to pull up the numbers." She directed the AV team to get her to the right spot and in the blink of an eye avoided what could have been a train-derailing kind of situation. A few minutes later a regional lead asked a tough question. She brought her energy up a notch. "Great question. Are you asking about timing or scope?" Then she answered the question that mattered.

It wasn't flawless. She slipped up on one metric and doubled back to correct it. But the room got what it needed: clarity, decisions, next steps. When she closed, she hit the last line on her card and walked off to that hopeful buzz, the hum that says people know what to do.

Later she told me she never felt "ready." But she felt steady. That was the difference. She didn't become someone else; she leaned on a few basics anyone can use: a first and last line on a card, feet-breath-eyes, an anchor face, one recovery sentence, a plain three-bullet spine. People told her she looked confident. She wasn't faking. She was present. And presence is a skill you can practice long before your brain decides you're "ready."

Training Yourself to Step into the Moment

Actors, athletes, and musicians don't wait to feel confident. They train for it. Actors rehearse lines until they become second nature. Athletes simulate high-pressure moments in practice. Musicians perform in small settings to get comfortable before stepping onto bigger stages. This kind of preparation builds confidence through repetition, making it easier to step into the moment despite nerves.

But preparation is only part of the equation. The most confident performers also master a crucial mental skill: controlling their own narratives.

Sports psychologist Nate Zinsser, author of *The Confident Mind*, points out that elite athletes don't simply prepare physically; they train their brains to expect success. Take a basketball player on a shooting streak. He feels unstoppable. His hands work like magic; the hoop stretches wide as an ocean, and he could drain a three-pointer blindfolded. Statistically, he's due to miss, but does he care? Nope. That ball is going in because the universe owes him one.

Meanwhile, when he's missed ten shots in a row? He's still convinced that the next one is a sure thing. Is this logical? No. Does it work? Without question. That's the point. Confidence isn't about reality—it's about momentum.

This isn't a delusion. It's a strategy. The best athletes, performers, and high achievers understand self-doubt is only one possible storyline. So they choose a better one. They focus on past wins, visualize success, and override hesitation with action.

The same principle applies beyond the stage or the court. Confidence in any setting, whether at work, in social situations, or tackling personal challenges is about choosing to believe in your own momentum before the proof is actually there.

Confidence Has a Body Language

Confidence is a set of repeatable behaviors that signal to yourself and to others that you belong in the moment.

Think about it. The most confident people in any setting, whether on stage, in a meeting, or at a social event, are not free of self-doubt. They have trained their bodies and minds to show up in a way that reads as confidence.

What does that look like in practice?

- **In sports:** Walking onto the court like you have already won the match when you may feel shaky inside. Returning a serve with full force instead of hesitating. Trusting the hours of training you have put in.
- **In professional settings:** Speaking at a steady pace when your heart is racing. Holding eye contact instead of looking down. Taking a breath before answering a question instead of rushing to fill the silence.
- **In social situations:** Standing with open body language instead of crossing your arms. Asking a question instead of waiting for someone to engage you. Smiling and nodding when you are feeling unsure.

None of these behaviors require you to feel confident first. When you do them consistently, your brain catches up. You build confidence in your performance, the kind that carries you through moments of doubt, that allows you to step forward when self-criticism creeps in.

Steady Beats Ready

My marketing vice president friend did not step onto the main stage because she felt that she owned it. She stepped into the spotlight because she had trained her mind and body for it.

That's the key. Confidence is not something you wait for—it's something you practice.

Instead of asking, *What if I fail?* reframe the question: *What if I show up and see what happens?*

That is all confidence is: a commitment to staying in the moment regardless of how ready you feel. I have experienced this firsthand.

A quarterly business review (QBR) is what it sounds like—a high-stakes meeting in which executives gather to review your team's performance, scrutinize the numbers, and ask pointed questions that may or may not make you reconsider all your life choices.

QBRs are common in corporate settings (such as sales, finance, and tech departments) in which teams present their results to senior leadership. In theory, these meetings are about alignment and strategy. They often feel like intense job interviews you didn't realize you signed up for. You're expected not only to present your results but also to defend them on the spot, in front of decision-makers who control budgets, promotions, and sometimes job security.

I've seen careers take off because of a strong QBR presentation. I've also seen people walk into one thinking it was another meeting—only to find out it was their last. Not one person but multiple people.

The first time I presented at a QBR, I felt certain they would expose me as an imposter. I arrived early because I needed time to sweat through my first shirt before anyone else showed up. The room was chilly, but somehow I was still overheating. I double-checked my slides, rehearsed my introduction in my head, and wondered if faking an emergency exit would tank my career.

Then the executives filed in. I tried to exude confidence, but my face said, "I've made a terrible mistake."

I launched into my presentation at twice the normal speed, gripping the podium like a life raft. Then came the questions.

"Can you walk us through the variance on slide seven?"

My mind went blank. I had looked at that slide a hundred times and told myself that they would ask about this one. Yet here I was, staring at it as though it had appeared out of thin air. I stumbled through an answer, my voice cracking, my brain screaming. *Well, this is it. This is how they find out.*

When the meeting ended, I all but sprinted out of the room, convinced that I had tanked my entire career.

Despite the mental certainty of death, I survived. As much as I wanted to erase that experience from my memory, I knew I had to face another QBR in three months.

So I decided the next time I was going to do better.

By my second QBR, I had changed my approach. Instead of memorizing slides, I practiced answering questions out loud. I paid attention to how I carried myself, adjusted my posture, and slowed my pacing.

By my third QBR, something had shifted. No longer trying to survive, I led the conversation with confidence. Carrying myself with more presence, I adjusted my pacing and reframed the moment as a discussion rather than a test. Knowing the material well enough to go without notes, I spoke at a steady pace. When someone challenged my numbers, there was no panic. I gave a nod and a calm response: "That's a great question. Let's walk through it."

At one point I made a joke. It was a planned joke, not a nervous, rambling attempt at humor. They laughed.

That was when I found out: I wasn't surviving these meetings anymore—I was in control of them.

"I've Got This" Energy

Looking back, I realize that the biggest shift wasn't that I had become a gifted speaker. It was that I had practiced the core behaviors of confidence (posture, pacing, and reframing) until they became my default. I had learned a few simple but powerful techniques that made all the difference:

1. **Posture and presence**. In my first QBR my body language screamed insecurity. By the third, I had learned that standing tall, keeping my shoulders open, and making eye contact made me feel more confident (despite not actually believing it yet).
2. **Pacing and silence**. I stopped rushing through my words and started using pauses to my advantage. Pausing makes you look more in control while you are still figuring out what to say next.
3. **Reframing the moment**. Instead of seeing the QBR as a test in which I had to prove my worth, I started seeing it as a conversation. My job was not to defend myself but rather to lead the discussion.

The Takeaway

Confidence does not come from waiting until you feel ready. It comes from showing up, adjusting, and learning from each experience.

By my third QBR, I had not eliminated all my nerves, but I had learned how to manage them. I had learned how to step into the moment with presence, to own the space I was in, and to lead the conversation.

And once you do that, whether in a meeting, a performance, or any other high-pressure moment, you stop worrying about whether you belong.

You prove to yourself that you do.

Command the Room (without World Domination Vibes)

There are two kinds of people who bring up *The 48 Laws of Power* in conversation: (1) those hoping to get a handle on the invisible power rules everyone else seems to know and (2) those plotting world domination.

Robert Greene's book is infamous for its ruthless Machiavellian strategies designed to crush opponents. And yes, some of its advice leans into manipulation. For those of us who find these tactics foreign, it can be an eye-opening guide to understanding how power works.

Not everyone plays fairly. Some people use tactics that prioritize self-interest over ethics. Learning how power operates doesn't mean you have to use it for manipulation. It means you can recognize when it's being used *on you.* In that sense, *The 48 Laws of Power* isn't only a playbook for influence but is a survival guide for navigating the competitive, often-less-than-altruistic arenas of the world.

Like it or not, we all navigate power dynamics, whether in meetings, social settings, or family gatherings in which one relative insists on controlling the holiday menu like a medieval king. The good news? You don't need manipulation to command a room. But you can learn from how people respond to confidence and presence.

So let's take a few of the non-evil lessons from *The 48 Laws of Power* and put them to good use.

Strategy 1: Court Attention (without Being Loud)

Robert Greene talks about commanding attention, not by being the loudest voice in the room but by being intentional about how you present yourself. Think about the most interesting people you have encountered. They were not the ones shouting over everyone else. Instead, they carried themselves in a way that made people pay attention.

Presence is about being noticed with purpose, drawing it in a way that makes people want to listen.

Here is how you can do that:

- **Adjust your body language**. People often judge confidence based on body language. Stand tall, avoid fidgeting, and make purposeful movements. Someone who carries himself or herself with ease appears more in control.
- **Use vocal clarity**. Ever notice how people lean in when someone speaks slow with deliberation? Rushing through your words makes you sound nervous, while a steady, clear voice commands respect.
- **Control your space**. If you are standing, do not shift your weight. If seated, avoid shrinking into your chair. Minor adjustments in posture can change how others perceive your authority.

The best way to build this skill is to practice presence in low-stakes situations. The next time you order coffee, do it with intention, stand with confidence, make clear eye contact, and speak at a steady pace. These small habits build over time, making it easier to carry that same energy into high-pressure situations.

Strategy 2: Enter Action with Boldness

Hesitation is like blood in the water for self-doubt. The moment you start second-guessing yourself, your brain leaps into action, creating a highlight reel of every mistake you have ever made. Imposter syndrome thrives in the gap between thinking and acting.

That is why boldness is often mistaken for competence. People assume that those who step forward with confidence know what they are doing. Sometimes they are just as unsure as the rest of us.

This does not mean you should charge with recklessness. It means you should train yourself to act before self-doubt has time to take hold.

One way to do this is through the Bold First Step method:

- If you're in a meeting and have an idea, speak up within three seconds of thinking about it. The longer you wait, the more time your brain has to talk you out of it.
- If you're at a networking event, introduce yourself to the first person you make eye contact with. Don't hover awkwardly by the drinks table, waiting for the perfect moment.
- If you're in a social setting such as a party or group gathering, start a conversation before overthinking it. Compliment someone's outfit, ask about his or her drink, or say, "How do you know the host?" (No need for groundbreaking dialogue. Get the words out before your brain convinces you to retreat to the snack table.)

The goal is to train your brain to act before hesitation derails you.

Strategy 3: Control the Frame

Whoever controls the framing of a discussion (how it's structured) holds the most sway. This does not mean dominating the discussion. It means being intentional about how you guide it.

Walk into a meeting thinking, *I hope I don't mess this up,* and you'll find yourself on the defensive. Shift that to *Here's what I want to communicate,* and everything changes.

You can apply this to any interaction:

- **Before a meeting, set a mental frame.** Don't ask, *What if I fail?* Ask, *What do I want people to take away from this?*

- **Use questions to steer a conversation**. Instead of waiting to react, take the lead by asking thoughtful questions that shift the discussion in a direction where you feel most confident.
- **Reframe moments of doubt**. If you catch yourself thinking, *I don't belong here,* replace it with *I bring value to this room because . . .* and fill in the blank. Your brain will believe what you tell it.

The best way to practice this skill is through a pre-meeting reframe exercise. Before any high-stakes conversation, take a few minutes to decide:

- What is the key message I want to convey?
- What questions can I ask to guide the discussion?
- What will I focus on instead of my self-doubt?

This small shift can make a major difference in how you show up.

The Bottom Line

You do not need to be the loudest person in the room to be the most respected. You do not need to feel 100 percent confident to step into a moment with presence.

By practicing presence, acting with boldness, and learning to control the frame of a conversation, you can step into any space with a sense of ownership, despite self-doubt trying to hold you back.

The best part? The more you do it, the less you must pretend. Because you prove to yourself that you belong.

What a Teen Fiddle Prodigy Taught Me about Belonging

Old-time music jams are supposed to be low pressure, inclusive, and welcoming. They are not competitions. Nobody is handing out trophies for the fastest fiddler or the most impressive banjo break. Yet for years I approached these jams with a level of anxiety reserved for job interviews and annual cholesterol screenings.

The problem was not the jam itself. It was the story I told myself about where I fit in.

I convinced myself that because I was not the best musician in the room, I should play quietly, stay out of the way, and not draw too much attention to my playing. I watched others take the lead and assumed that was their role, not mine. Instead of enjoying the music, I spent most of my time comparing myself to others and concluding that I was falling short. It's the same lying mind we met back in chapter 3, still running its tired playbook.

Then came the night I almost let my self-doubt push me out of the circle.

There is nothing quite like watching a teenager be better at something you have spent decades practicing. It is a humbling experience. That night a fourteen-year-old fiddler showed up to the jam. He was one of Ben's students, the same Ben we met back in chapter 11 and a close friend of mine. He is the most generous ambassador of Appalachian music I've ever known. He's taught countless players, produced my album, and we've written songs together. If anyone understands the heart of a jam circle, it's him. That night his young student was stealing the show.

I was spiraling.

The old script started running in my head: *You have been at this for years, and you are still not at his level. What does that say about you?* I felt myself shrinking, playing more softly, fading into the background. At one point I considered putting my instrument down and sitting out the rest of the night.

Then I noticed something.

As I sat there, lost in my self-doubt, I started paying attention to the rest of the circle.

Not everyone was playing lead melodies at lightning speed. Some musicians were holding a steady rhythm. Some were adding soft harmonies. Some were tapping their feet and nodding along.

I realized a jam isn't about proving your worth. It's about playing your part.

The fourteen-year-old might have been the most technically skilled musician there, but that didn't make everyone else irrelevant. Rhythm players kept the song grounded, while harmony players added depth. The guy in the corner, chiming in on only half the songs, still contributed to the music.

I struggled to justify my presence in the jam, as if I needed to prove my worthiness. Nobody was grading my performance. Nobody was waiting for me to impress them.

They were playing music. I could either sit there analyzing my inadequacy or I could pick up my instrument and play.

That night, instead of measuring myself against the young prodigy, I listened with curiosity. Watching his technique became an opportunity to learn rather than compare. After he finished the tune, I asked if he could slow it down so I could try it. Shifting my focus, I began paying attention to how my playing could complement the group rather than worrying about whether I measured up to the best player in the room.

That shift from comparison to curiosity and contribution changed everything.

I played with more confidence, not because I believed I was great but because I stopped believing that greatness was a requirement for participation. I started enjoying the music again.

When I engaged, when I played with confidence, when I stopped shrinking, the jam sounded better. The rhythm felt stronger. The energy lifted. The experience became more enjoyable, not only for me but also for everyone else in the room.

Maybe you have never sat in a music circle, quietly judging your own abilities. But I bet you have had moments when you convinced yourself you did not belong.

Maybe it's at work when you assume you need to outwork everyone else before you add value to the project.

Maybe it's in social situations when you hold back from engaging because you think you are not as interesting or charismatic as the people around you.

Maybe it's in a creative pursuit when you hesitate to share your work because you think it is not as good as what others are doing.

In almost every setting there are different roles to play. The best leader in a meeting is not always the one with the flashiest ideas but is often the person who listens well and connects the dots. The best conversationalist is not the one who talks the most but is the one who makes others feel heard. The best team member is not always the most talented but is often the one who makes others better by showing up and contributing.

You Do Not Have to Be the Best—You Just Have to Show Up

The biggest lie that imposter syndrome tells us is that we must earn our place in the room, that we must prove our worth before we deserve to take part.

You do not have to be the best to belong.

You do not have to have the perfect answer to contribute.

You do not have to wait until you feel confident to take up space.

You must show up, engage, and trust that your presence adds something valuable.

Confidence Is a Habit, Not a Destination

If confidence were a place, we would all be typing it into Google Maps, hoping for turn-by-turn directions ("In 500 feet merge onto Self-Assurance Parkway. Your destination will be on the right.")

Confidence isn't the final stop where you unpack your bags and live happily ever after. It's more like a gym membership, something you must keep working on, including the days you would rather stay on the couch eating chips.

Confidence is a muscle. The more you use it the stronger it gets.

Every time you step into a room with presence, you rewrite the script in your head. Every time you raise your hand in a meeting, speak up in a conversation, or resist the urge to shrink, you reinforce the message: *I belong here.*

Confidence grows through action, not grand gestures. You don't need to deliver a TED (technology, entertainment, design) talk, conquer Mount Everest, or stride into a room as if Beyoncé's wind machine follows you everywhere. It takes shape in small everyday moments.

It's ordering food without rehearsing your order five times in your head.

It's resisting the urge to apologize before making a reasonable request.

It's realizing that most people are too busy worrying about themselves to scrutinize your every move.

These moments add up. Over time they establish how you see yourself.

Your Challenge: Step into Confidence

Since confidence is something you do, not something you have, here's your mission:

1. **Find one moment this week to step into confidence**. Speak up, take up space, or try something that feels outside your comfort zone.

2. **Reframe one self-doubt thought before a big moment**. Instead of *I'm not ready for this*, try *I'm learning as I go, and that's enough*. Instead of *They're going to see right through me*, try *I have something valuable to contribute*.

3. **Celebrate the progress, even if it's just showing up**. This is one for the Greatest Hits & Misses journal. Confidence isn't about perfection. It's about participation. If you walked into the room, spoke up, or didn't talk yourself out of an opportunity, you won.

Remember: Confidence isn't a place you arrive—it's a habit you build daily. Some days you'll feel unstoppable. Other days you'll want to crawl under a blanket and never come out. But if you keep showing up, something surprising happens.

You stop faking it.

You realize you were never an imposter to begin with.

Because confidence isn't about performing for others. It's about showing up as you—and trusting that's enough.

CONCLUSION

The Real You Was Never an Imposter

If you're worried that you're not good enough, congratulations: *You are.*

That's the catch-22 of imposter syndrome. The fear that you don't belong? It shows up when you're doing something meaningful, stretching yourself, or stepping into unfamiliar territory. You feel like a fraud not because you're unqualified but because you care.

And yet imposter syndrome has a way of twisting that truth against us. It whispers, *If you were good enough, you wouldn't feel this way.* It convinces us that confidence should be effortless, that certainty is a prerequisite for belonging.

That's the lie. As we've explored throughout this book, confidence isn't about never doubting yourself again. It's about learning how to move forward despite the doubt.

This is the final and most important shift.

You don't need to "fix" yourself. There was never anything wrong with you.

Confidence isn't about erasing self-doubt. It's about learning to work with it, to step forward anyway, to trust that the real you, the version that's been here all along, is more than enough.

You don't have to wait for permission to take up space.

You don't have to earn your place at the table.

You must recognize that you were *never* an imposter.

That changes everything.

Turns Out You're Human

If you picked up this book hoping for a step-by-step guide to erase self-doubt, I have some bad news: That was never the goal.

Imposter syndrome isn't a problem to "fix" because it's not a sign that something is wrong. It's a sign that you care. You're stretching yourself. You're stepping into spaces that challenge you. That's a good thing.

The real mistake isn't feeling like an imposter. It's believing that confidence means never feeling that way again. Confidence does not erase self-doubt—it's the ability to move forward despite it.

Think of the people you admire, the ones who seem self-assured. Do you think they've never been uncertain about anything? Of course they have. They've learned that self-doubt isn't a stop sign. It's background noise. The real question isn't how to get rid of imposter syndrome—it's how to work with it.

That's been the goal of this book, not to erase that voice in your head but to teach you how to respond to it; not to eliminate fear but to help you walk through it. Self-doubt doesn't mean you don't belong—it means you're human.

If I could go back and talk to my past selves: the boy blinded by the Big Sandy lights at the state wrestling tournament, the young professional stuttering through his first sales call, the aspiring musician struggling to find the right intonation on the fiddle, the grown man convinced that confidence was a magical trait other people were born with, I know what I would say.

I would tell them, *You're not an imposter. You never were.*

I would remind them that the fear of being "found out" wasn't proof they didn't belong. It was proof they cared, that every person they admired had moments of doubt too, but they kept showing up anyway.

I would tell them this: *Nothing is waiting on the other side of imposter syndrome except your own decision to stop letting it control you.*

You already have what you need. You don't need more credentials, more experience, or some cosmic sign from the universe before you're "allowed" to take up space. You have always belonged. You must decide to believe it.

Imposter syndrome will try creeping back in because that's what it does. Next time it whispers, *What if you're not good enough?* you'll have an answer ready:

What if I am?

Because the real you—the one who shows up, keeps going and refuses to let doubt call the shots—was never an imposter, and never will be.

The title of this book is *I Can't Believe They Let Me In.* That's a lie too.

Nobody "let you in."

No one gave you an accidental golden ticket. You didn't sneak past the gate while no one was looking. You belong here. You always have.

Imposter syndrome will try to convince you otherwise. It will whisper that you got lucky, that everyone else has figured out, that you're one step away from being exposed. But now you know the truth. Everyone is figuring it out as they go. The ones who succeed? They're not the ones who never doubt themselves. They're the ones who step forward anyway. So, take the shot.

Introspection

Now that you know you belong, what will you do with it?
Where will you step next?
Go do something about it—something only you can do.

REFERENCES

Sources Referenced

A River Runs Through It, by Norman Maclean

Catch-22, by Joseph Heller

The Confident Mind, by Nate Zinsser

The Exorcist, by William Peter Blatty

The Great Gatsby, by F. Scott Fitzgerald

Grit, by Angela Duckworth

Hamilton, by Lin-Manuel Miranda (Stage musical)

The Inner Game of Tennis, by W. Timothy Gallwey

Jurassic Park, by Michael Crichton

The Laws of Human Nature, by Robert Greene

Quiet, by Susan Cain

Rocky, starring Sylvester Stallone (film)

Yes Please, by Amy Poehler

SpongeBob SquarePants, created by Stephen Hillenburg (animated TV series)

Storming Heaven, by Denise Giardina

Talent Is Overrated, by Geoff Colvin

Talladega Nights: The Ballad of Ricky Bobby, directed by Adam McKay (film)

The 100-Year-Old Man Who Climbed Out the Window and Disappeared, by Jonas Jonasson

The Power of Now, by Eckhart Tolle

To Kill a Mockingbird, by Harper Lee

What Makes Sammy Run, by Budd Schulberg

The 48 Laws of Power, by Robert Greene

Famous People Referenced

Adele

Ali, Muhammad

Angelou, Maya

Armstrong, Neil

Biles, Simone

Bowie, David

Brown, Brené

Churchill, Winston

Christie, Agatha

Darwin, Charles

Def Leppard

Disney, Walt

Duckworth, Angela

Einstein, Albert

Fleck, Béla

Gaiman, Neil

Gaga, Lady

Giddens, Rhiannon

Hopper, Grace

Iron Maiden

Jordan, Michael

Joyner-Kersee, Jackie

Kahlo, Frida

King, Billie Jean

King, Stephen

Miranda, Lin-Manuel

Obama, Barack

Winfrey, Oprah

Poehler, Amy

The Police

Prine, John

Rowling, J. K.

Sandberg, Sheryl

Schultz, Howard

Steinbeck, John

U2

Van Gogh, Vincent

Williams, Serena

Jobs, Steve

Joan of Arc

Alexander the Great

ACKNOWLEDGMENTS

This book weaves together my story with the voices, lessons, and music of the people who have shaped me along the way. I'm deeply grateful to Patrick Price, whose developmental insights helped shape the structure and soul of this book, and to Jonathan Wright, whose meticulous copyediting refined every line with care and precision.

To my colleagues and mentors throughout my entire career—thank you for teaching me more than numbers or strategy ever could. You showed me what leadership, resilience, and empathy look like in the real world. I've learned from every one of you, and many of your lessons are woven through these pages.

To my friends in the West Virginia fiddle and old-time music community, including Ben Townsend, Dave Asti, Chris Haddox, and countless others who handed me tunes, encouragement, and patience—thank you. You reminded me that music isn't about perfection; it's about persistence, joy, and community.

To my family and friends who continue to endure my musical practice sessions (banjo twangs, squeaky fiddle notes, and all) and my often messy journey through life, I owe you more than I can put on a page.

To my wife, Julie. You are the absolute best thing that has ever happened to me, and I am so thankful to have found you so early in life. I love you and the life we have built together.

And to everyone who ever nudged me to keep writing, keep playing, and keep showing up—this book exists because of you.

ABOUT THE AUTHOR

CC Nichols builds teams, launches life-saving therapies, and helps people tell themselves a better story. For over two decades he has worked across the rare-disease landscape, leading regional organizations through high-stakes launches, coaching field leaders across large territories, and shaping cultures in which people can do their best work. His experience spans product launch, market development, training, medical education, and national key-opinion-leader strategy.

Before he led teams, he carried a bag and worked the front lines. Those early years still inform his approach to presence: Start strong, speak plainly, and keep moving when the moment gets loud. Colleagues know him for calmness under pressure, clear communication, and a bias for useful action over theater.

CC is a U.S. Navy veteran who was deployed to the Southwest Asia theater of operations during the Gulf War era. He holds a master of business administration degree and a bachelor of science degree in economics from West Virginia University. Off the clock he's a songwriter and performer who believes live music is proof that courage and imperfection can share a stage. He and his wife live in the area where they grew up: Mineral County, West Virginia.

www.ingramcontent.com/pod-product-compliance
Lightning Source LLC
Chambersburg PA
CBHW060418130626
46555CB00005B/2123